RUMPHIUS' ORCHIDS

Rumphius' Orchids

Orchid Texts from *The Ambonese Herbal*

by Georgius Everhardus Rumphius

Translated, edited, annotated,

and with an introduction by

E. M. Beekman

YALE UNIVERSITY PRESS

NEW HAVEN AND LONDON

Support for publication of this book includes a grant to the author
by the Lounsbery Foundation through the University of Massachusetts.

Frontispiece: This is the only known portrait drawn from life. Rumphius' son, Paulus
Augustus, drew the likeness sometime between October 1695 and July of 1696 in Kota
Ambon, about six years before his father's death. The print states that Rumphius was
sixty-eight when he posed for this portrait, and that the governor then in office wrote
the Latin encomium. This was Nicolaes Schaghen, who was Ambon's governor from 1691
to 1696. The Latin verse reads in translation: "Though he be blind, his mental eyes are so
sharp that no one can best him at inquiry or discernment. Rumphius is a German by
birth but his loyalty and pen are completely Dutch. Let the work say the rest."

Designed by Nancy Ovedovitz and set in Monotype Centaur type
by Tseng Information Systems. Printed in the United States of America
by Edwards Brothers, Inc.

Library of Congress Cataloging-in-Publication Data
Rumpf, Georg Eberhard, 1627–1702.
[Amboinsche kruidboek. English] Rumphius' orchids : orchid texts from The Ambonese
herbal / Georgius Everhardus Rumphius ; translated, edited, annotated, and with an
introduction by E. M. Beekman.   p. cm.   Includes bibliographical references (p.).
ISBN 0-300-09814-6 (cloth : alk. paper)   1. Orchids—Indonesia—Ambon Island.
2. Rumpf, Georg Eberhard, 1627–1702.   3. Botany—Pre-Linnean works.
I. Beekman, E. M., 1939–
II. Title.   QK495.O64R7913   2003   584′.4′09598—dc21   2002041161

A catalogue record for this book is available from the British Library.
The paper in this book meets the guidelines for permanence and durability
of the Committee on Production Guidelines for Book Longevity
of the Council on Library Resources.

10   9   8   7   6   5   4   3   2   1

In Memoriam
Rob Nieuwenhuys
and
Henk de Wit

To him who keeps an Orchis' heart
The swamps are pink in June.
Emily Dickinson

Faire catleya.
Marcel Proust

CONTENTS

CONTENTS

LIST OF ORIGINAL PLATES
but with Modern Binomials

ACKNOWLEDGMENTS

The present volume constitutes a modest installment of the larger enterprise, which is to produce an annotated translation of Rumphius' entire *Amboinsche Kruidboek* (Ambonese Herbal). The Richard Lounsbery Foundation made it possible for me to get the project off the ground; their generosity gave me a running start, and I very much appreciate their faith in me. I particularly want to thank Marta Norman for her kindness and professionalism. The work now continues under the auspices of The National Tropical Botanical Garden.

These orchid texts are offered in appreciation to Lynn Margulis, who, with deliberate affection, steered me in the right direction.

This book would not exist without Bart Eaton's constant care and support. He was the first to suggest that I gather Rumphius' orchid texts into a separate book, and I hope we did Susanna proud. He came to the rescue when rebarbative intrusions almost scuttled the present enterprise. Mr. Eaton's generosity was seconded by Catherine Rodriguez and Juliet Possati. I am grateful for their loyalty.

Explanatory illustrations are crucial in a text like this, if only to prove that Rumphius' analogies and similes are quite correct. Locating examples, not to mention acquiring permission for reproduction, is one of the most frustrating experiences one encounters when dealing with what are, oxymoronically, called "public services." I am, therefore, in debt to my indefatigable friend Dr. E. M. Joon, who also knows how hard it is to breach Holland's *takenpaketten:* defenses denser than any medieval fortress. I thank him for trying.

To make sure that this would be a responsible text, I enlisted the aid of several specialists. Mr. J. B. Comber, expert on Indonesian orchids, corrected the binomials I derived from J. J. Smith's work published in the beginning of the twentieth century. I also profited greatly from the expertise of the orchidologist Joseph Arditti, Professor of Biology Emeritus, University of California at Irvine.

Dr. Henk van der Werff, of the Missouri Botanical Garden, scrutinized these orchid texts and offered useful commentary. But he has done more than that: he became my indispensable guide through the technical jungle, and I hope he will remain my botanical cicerone for a long time to come. I am truly grateful for his selfless commitment to the larger project.

When the need arose my friend and ally Dr. H. Heestermans came through with some crucial material. As he has always done.

In order to make this volume complete, I needed reproductions of the plates from the first edition. I am grateful to the Universiteitsbibliotheek of Leiden University and its director, Dr. R. Breugelmans, for granting permission to reproduce the sixteen plates from the first edition of Rumphius' *Amboinsche Kruidboek.*

Some of the people mentioned above know how my fortune has changed and immediately volunteered to help as much as possible. I would like to take this opportunity to thank them as well as my other loyal friends who boost, if not my immune system, my resolve to complete this quixotic venture. Keep me steady and on course.

E. M. Beekman

INTRODUCTION

The orchid is no longer a sinister and decadent passion but rather a commodity that represents a $9 billion business worldwide.[1] This democratization took place in less than two centuries. Orchid fever, or orchidelirium, began in Europe in the nineteenth century, and the craze was in some ways comparable to the Dutch tulipomania of the seventeenth. But it lasted longer. The British leisure class contracted the fever in 1818, when the first *Cattleya labiata* bloomed in Suffolk.[2] In 1913, Marcel Proust translated the same plant into a new verb that conjugated making love at its most intoxicating (*faire catleya*).[3] The mania was cured by the reality of the First World War and did not reappear in the United States and Europe until the last quarter of the twentieth century. By then the erstwhile rapture had been replaced by an often vicious commercial enterprise.[4]

Why did it take Westerners so long to contract orchid fever? After all, the orchid had been in bloom 100 to 110 million years before the present[5] and it belongs to the most ubiquitous and variable of plant families, ranging in habitat from Alaska to Tierra del Fuego, and in size from a couple of millimeters (*Platystele*) to a plant mass of a ton (*Grammatophyllum speciosum*).

It is the largest plant family on earth; Dressler is certain of 725 genera and 19,192 species, adding that "a figure between 20,000 and 25,000 orchid species seems reasonable."[6] The plant is present in almost every climate zone in Europe, with the largest number of these temperate species living in the Mediterranean basin, the center of European antiquity. And indeed, the orchid (a Greek word for "testicle") was briefly mentioned by Hippocrates (fifth century B.C.), then Theophrastus (who was the first to use the noun *orchid*) and Dioscorides, succeeded by the Romans, especially Pliny and Galen, then Arab botanists, into the Renaissance,[7] to be followed by the great explosion of botanical study in the seventeenth century with Holland at its center. Every European country had its wild orchids; for instance, even such an unlikely place as the Netherlands harbors twenty-eight species.[8] And yet it was not until the nineteenth century that the orchid insinuated itself into the Western imagination. The intimation came from the tropics.

Asia had cherished the orchid much earlier than Europe, with China antedating everyone else. The earliest mention of orchids in the world is said to be in the Chinese "Book of Songs" which dates from about the tenth to the sixth century B.C.[9] Whereas in Western literature, the orchid was, generally speaking, associated with salaciousness and the melodramatic (for instance in the second chapter of Raymond Chandler's *The Big Sleep*),[10] in China, Japan, and in Asia as a whole the orchid was justly lauded for its fragrance and its potential medicinal virtues. Rumphius too had nothing sinister to say about these plants, but praised them for their bootless beauty. But the European imagination was provoked only when it was finally introduced to a tropical species.

More than three-quarters of known orchid species are tropical, and about three-quarters of all species are epiphytes, that is to say they live on but not from trees. Epiphytes are "limited to tropical and subtropical environments";[11] there are no epiphytes in Europe. The huge landmasses of North America and Eurasia know relatively few orchid species: 75 genera and 817 species. Australasia has the next fewest species, then tropical Africa. Most orchid genera and orchid species are found in tropical America (306 genera and 8,266 known species), with tropical Asia second: 250 genera and 6,800 known species.[12] In other words, more than two-thirds of the world's orchid genera and species are from tropical America and Asia, and yet Western knowledge of tropical orchids was extremely limited until the nineteenth century. There are very few classics in the literature of Asian orchidology, and even those few are virtually unknown. As an example, Rumphius' classic texts were not translated into a vernacular language until the present volume.

The first tropical orchid introduced to Europe was the vanilla orchid (*Vanilla planifolia* from Mexico). The fruits of *tlilxochitl* (*tlilli* means "black" in Nahuatl, and *xóchitl* is "flower")[13] flavored Emperor Montezuma's favored chocolate drink. Although Spaniards brought knowledge of this orchid to Europe in the early sixteenth century, it was the Dutch who established it in botanical literature. Clusius, a botanist from the southern Netherlands, "published the first botanical notice of a *Vanilla* species"[14] in 1605, while the first use of the noun that established it as generic nomenclature was by Willem Piso (1611–1678),[15] the Dutch physician who accompanied Johan Maurits von Nassau-Siegen to Brazil. Johan Maurits' gubernatorial group of 46 scholars and artists assembled a natural history of Brazil—*Historia Naturalis Brasiliae,* published in 1648—that remained unsurpassed for a very long time. This seminal text, compiled by Piso, was planned and executed during the Dutch West Indies Company's abortive attempt to establish a permanent Dutch colony in South America, roughly between 1630 and 1657. Clusius and Piso were not the only Dutch botanists to establish tropical orchids in the West. "The first tropical orchid cultivated in Europe was figured in Paul Hermann's *Paradisus Batavus* (1698) as the American *Epidendrum nodosum* (*Brassavola nodosa*). The plant, listed as *Epidendrum corassavicum folio crasso sulcato,* was grown in the garden of Casper Fagel, having been introduced into Holland from Curaçao."[16] Paul Hermann (1646–1695) was considered the best botanist residing in the Dutch Republic during the seventeenth century, Fagel was a high official and intimate of the Dutch ruling family, while Curaçao, captured in 1634, had become the central depot for Dutch trade in the Caribbean after 1650.

The Dutch presence in Asia was more permanent, especially in Southeast Asia. It is true that the literature of tropical botany begins with the Portuguese, especially the great Garcia da Orta (?1490–?1570) who lived in Goa, India, and inspired Camoens' epic, *The Lusiad,* a poem that included a beautiful eulogy of the Moluccas. After him comes the Cape Verdean

Cristóbal Acosta (1525–1594), who repeated a great deal from Orta in his *Treatise Concerning the Drugs and Medicines of the East Indies* published in Burgos in 1578, followed by the Spanish physician Nicolas Monardes (1493–1588), who published a treatise on medicinal plants from tropical America in 1574 in Seville. One should probably add the *Natural History of the West Indies,* published in Toledo in 1526, by Gonzalo Fernandez de Oviedo (1478–1557), which also discussed nature in the Americas. However, the work of Orta, Monardes, and Acosta gained widespread professional renown only after the Flemish botanist Clusius — Charles de l'Escluse (1526–1609) — published their work in Latin epitomes in 1567, 1574, and 1582. They were republished in a single volume in 1593 and reprinted in a collective edition, *Exoticorum libri decem,* published in 1605. Most of the scholars and natural historians of the seventeenth century, including Rumphius, knew these works only through Clusius' Latin translations.

The Iberian triad was most definitely surpassed by the Dutch trio of Jacobus Bontius (1592–1631), Hendrik Adriaan van Reede tot Drakenstein (1636–1691), and Georgius Everhardus Rumphius (1627–1702). The work of these three pioneers was based on first-hand observation in, respectively, Java, India's Malabar coast, and eastern Indonesia. Bontius' work was even shorter than that of Monardes and Acosta, but Van Reede's *Hortus Malabaricus* and Rumphius' *Het Amboinsche Kruidboek* (The Ambonese Herbal) were voluminous enterprises — together the two works add up to nineteen folio volumes — that established themselves as the unsurpassed foundation of the study of tropical Asian botany.

During the seventeenth century, the Dutch Republic was the premier European center for botanical studies, especially tropical botany. By that time there was a considerable literature (including some discussion of orchids) on European botany, even on tropical American nature, but very little about Asian flora. The basic reason was ignorance. There had been no *regular* intercourse with Asia prior to the fifteenth century; Europeans knew about certain Asian commodities, to be sure, but only as *products.* They had not verified the botanical provenance for themselves. When information finally did trickle down to Europe it came most often in the form of scattered references in accounts of travel. There were few systematic descriptions of tropical flora before the eighteenth century, and the handful that do exist, such as Van Reede's herbal of India and Rumphius' of Indonesia, are pioneering texts of inestimable value. The territory they had discovered appeared limitless.

If we restrict this discussion to orchids alone, we can provide the following figures as examples. China has a total of 158 genera and 966 species of orchids.[17] "The orchid flora of southern China is closely related to that of Malaysia,"[18] hence we will find that some of the genera Rumphius discovered are also found in southern China. Mention of Malaysia brings to mind the tropical archipelago that is the natural habitat in this book. In terms of Indonesia, according to J. B. Comber, Java has 731 named orchid species,[19] Sumatra has just under 1,200 named species, and Borneo about 1,400.[20] In Papua New Guinea there are untold species. For example, in a few years during the first decade of the twentieth century, the German botanist Rudolf

Schlechter recorded 116 genera and 1,463 species, of which 1,102 species were new.[21] J. J. Smith listed 104 species for the small island of Ambon where Rumphius lived three-quarters of his life. Thirty-six of those species and four varieties were, according to Smith, endemic to Ambon, and 23 species were to be found only in the eastern archipelago.[22] Rumphius described or pictured about 36 confirmed species and 12 that are subject to taxonomic debate.[23] By contrast, Van Reede listed only six species of orchids in his *Hortus Malabaricus*, all epiphytes (which in the Malayalam language were called *maravara*) from the Malabar coast in western India.[24] Comber contends that a rough estimate of 5,000 species for all Indonesian orchids is not exaggerated.

That is a surfeit of orchids, far more than all the species and genera of Eurasia combined, yet this floral wealth was practically unknown in the seventeenth century. Van Reede's half a dozen Malabar orchids were not known to Rumphius: he never saw the twelfth and last volume of the *Hortus Malabaricus*, which discussed those *maravara*. Rumphius parades received knowledge rather perfunctorily in his first orchid chapter. It was not much to build on. At least Clusius and Dodonaeus printed brief descriptions of true orchids, but Rumphius never knew Gessner's drawing of orchid seed (though he does mention the Swiss botanist) because it was not published until 1751–1777. Rumphius includes Tragus and Kircher only because they posited a theory concerning the orchid's generation, despite the fact that this was still the prevalent myth that the plants were somehow generated from spilled animal semen, or by means of abiogenesis, which is spontaneous creation from carcasses.[25] Rumphius politely declined to support such fanciful notions and correctly intuited the presence of orchid seed, which he described as "wool," and correctly noted its dispersal by the wind. He also mentions the contemporary botanist Bauhin, who listed the wrong plant, and otherwise fell back on his main source and model, the Roman natural historian Pliny the Elder. One should note that thereafter Rumphius does not mention any other source because they were unavailable, and useless even if at hand. Rumphius was creating a fundamental classic while he wrote, pretty much alone, in relative intellectual isolation, on a remote island in Indonesia's eastern archipelago. Scientific study of the orchid family was not initiated until the nineteenth century.

An encounter with Rumphius, once dubbed "The Blind Seer of Ambon," be it the work or the man, is a privilege and a liberal education. He was born in late October or early November in 1627 in Wölfersheim, a small town in the approximate center of Hesse, some 25 miles north of Frankfurt.[26] His father, August Rumpf (?–1666), was a *Baumeister*, a combination architect and construction contractor, and his mother was Anna Elisabeth Keller (?1600–1651), who had family connections in the United Provinces, a republic now better known as the Kingdom of the Netherlands. Despite his German birthplace, Rumphius learned Dutch from his mother's family.

Georg Everhard Rumpf, whom I will call Rumphius for convenience sake, was born when the Thirty Years War had been raging for about a decade. The Rumpf family experienced the hazards of marauding soldiers, famine, plague epidemics, and the devastation of their region. Beginning as a brutal war of religion, the conflict gradually turned into a vicious political contest in which principles and ideologies became feckless accommodations. Since national fighting forces did not yet exist, the war was fought by hirelings. Mercenaries had no regard for territorial sanctity: they burned and pillaged and sacked with democratic fervor. The ruination of Hesse had one benefit: it provided Rumphius' father with steady employment. Local aristocrats needed to have their ancestral seats restored to former glory, and a man such as the elder Rumpf was in great demand. The only trouble was that his employers were broke and more often than not failed to pay him for his services so that, even though the war ensured that the Rumpf family would survive, it also made sure that it would suffer from a chronic lack of money.

Because of his father's social position Rumphius enjoyed the privilege of education. In the seventeenth century education was a luxury, not a right, and depended on one's ability to pay. As a young child in Wölfersheim he was taught Latin, Greek, and Hebrew by a private instructor. Rumphius' father taught the children of his aristocratic employers such things as drafting, mathematics, and the principles of construction, particularly building defensive structures such as redoubts and fortifications. Subjects like that were not taught in schools, so Rumphius was again lucky that he had a father who could instruct him in these skills. As a very young adolescent, not much older than ten or eleven, Rumphius went to the Gymnasium in Hanau, a city east of Frankfurt. The connection with Hanau is religious as well as economic (his father worked for the Counts of Hanau and later for the city itself). In 1597, Count Philipp Ludwig II invited Protestant refugees from the Spanish Netherlands to his domain, granting them a number of privileges. They proceeded to build a new town and made Hanau prosperous. Throughout his life, Rumphius would (inaccurately) claim Hanau as his native city.

The new town these Netherlandic Protestants built bore a striking resemblance to New Amsterdam on the island of Manhattan and to Kota Ambon in eastern Indonesia, a town where Rumphius was to spend the last decades of his life. All three were built according to a pragmatic grid of square blocks of houses with streets that crossed each other at right angles, arranged around a central area that truly was a square. This was not standard city planning at the time, but an innovative endeavor. Just recall medieval cities, which grew like coral reefs, by accretion.

Hanau could boast of an institution of advanced learning because the Counts of Hanau, as Reformed Protestants, were champions of education. The curriculum comprised the traditional liberal arts: grammar, rhetoric, logic, arithmetic, geometry (not algebra), music, and astronomy. In an unfinished autobiographical poem,[27] Rumphius informs us that despite his talent for mathematics, he preferred the humanities, the "Muses" as he called them, and that he wanted to explore the "secrets of Nature." Be that as it may, Minerva had to defer to Mars for many years to come.

Rumphius stated that he left Hanau in 1645 at eighteen because he wanted to see Italy. To realize this dream he signed up as a mercenary with a commander who was a son of one of August Rumpf's former employers. Because of this connection, both father Rumpf and his son trusted the recruiter, who said he was gathering hirelings for the Doge of Venice, troops that would fight the Turks on Crete. The recruitment pitch was a lie. The bizarre events of the next three years hide several mysteries in the story of Rumphius' life. Rumphius and his fellow Hessians were shipped to Holland and abandoned. Then they somehow were corralled once more and transported to Texel, an island off the northern coast of Holland where Dutch fleets rendezvoused before embarking on long voyages all across the globe. As Rumphius recounts in his poem, the hoodwinked band of hirelings became part of a force of 2,000 men who were crammed into three ships. Not until they were sailing through the Channel were they told that their destination was Brazil, evidently as part of an expeditionary force intended to relieve the beleaguered Dutch in northern Brazil.

But Rumphius never made it to South America either. His ship was either wrecked or captured off the coast of Portugal in 1646, and he spent the next three years in the country that was Holland's commercial and political rival. There is enough evidence to say that he was in Portugal from 1646 to 1649 and that he lived there as a soldier. Rumphius and his fellow Hessians were used by the Portuguese government as border troops. Like all mercenaries, they lived off the land and earned the contempt of the local citizens. In a letter from 1682 he mentions that they once gathered a Portuguese variety of parsley to be eaten as a salad "despite being pelted with slingshots."[28] There are scattered references to his "Portuguese peregrination," (5:250) as he called it, throughout his work. Whatever the particulars, there is no doubt that the three Portuguese years meant a stint in foreign military service.

How he managed to leave Portugal and how he got back to Hesse we do not know. It is certain that he was back in Hesse in the summer of 1649, just about one year after the Thirty Years War ended with the Treaty of Münster. This time Rumphius followed in the more prudent footsteps of his father, and found employment in Idstein, a town northwest of Frankfurt. He worked for the local count as a *Bauschreiber*, a lesser version of what his father's job entailed. A brief description of his duties illustrates why Rumphius was such a valuable asset for the Dutch when he went to the Indies. As a *Bauschreiber* he had to oversee construction crews and was their liaison with the castle hierarchy. He also produced working designs, what we would call blueprints, for whatever structure was under construction, or any other proposed project, and was contractually obliged to teach his employer's children, just as his father had done. In Rumphius' case this covered "Arithmetic, Geometry, Architecture and related Arts." The latter most likely were drawing and painting.

Rumphius lasted only a year and a half on this job. One reason he quit was given by his employer, the Count of Idstein: Rumphius had publicly remonstrated against the Count's prohibition of Calvinist church services. Dissenting behavior was dangerous at the time, so that it may have been foresighted when Rumphius disappeared. A more likely reason is that his mother died in December of 1651. His father needed him and called him home. Once he was back with his family, Georg discovered that his father was in serious financial trouble, and he left perhaps in order not to be a burden on his parent. Be that as it may, within a week after his mother's death, Rumphius had left Hanau and probably Hesse as well.

Once again Rumphius signed on as a soldier, this time with the VOC or the Dutch East India Company, the business enterprise that was the first multinational corporation of the modern era. (I will refer to it throughout this book either by the Dutch acronym or the metonymy "the Company.") Again, we do not know how he got to Holland or who helped him solicit for a position, but his mother's family was more than likely involved because he left Europe the day after Christmas 1652, as an *adelborst,* which a contemporary dictionary translates as "gentleman soldier"—a small but significant step up the social ladder. In July of 1653 Rumphius disembarked in the colonial capital called Batavia on the island of Java, and by the end of that year he arrived in the Moluccas in the far eastern archipelago as a member of a military force. He had just turned twenty-six. He spent the next forty-eight years of his life in those eastern islands and never saw Java, Hesse, or Europe again.

It was not unusual for a German to go to the Indies as

an employee of the VOC. The Dutch company needed man-power and the small nation could not supply it. During the time Rumphius signed on, about 65 percent of the soldiers were foreign, while 35 percent of mariners had been born outside the Netherlands. These percentages only increased during the eighteenth century. The greatest number of *Gastarbeiter* were German, and the major reason for that was the ruinous Thirty Years War. Rumphius was not much different from his compatriots except that he managed to advance beyond the military, which not many foreigners were able to do.

If one survived, the journey to Java truly was a "sea-change into something rich and strange." But one thing must have been familiar to the young man from Hanau. Old Batavia was also built according to a rectangular grid, like Hanau's New Town and New Amsterdam on the Hudson. The Dutch engineers straightened out the Ciliwung River and diverted it into bricked canals that flowed by seventeenth-century Dutch houses complete with small gardens. In other words, Rumphius walked into a Dutch town transplanted to the tropics, though outside this relatively small center of palm-lined canals one encountered the different modes of real Asian life in the several *kampongs,* or neighborhoods, inhabited by ethnic groups from all over the archipelago.

But life in the eastern archipelago was stranger still. The European presence seemed almost negligible in this vast domain of water and a few lonesome islands. Rumphius set out to transfer this largely undisclosed world onto paper, but first he had to survive the fortunes of war one more time. Yet again we lack details and official confirmation, but if one has had any familiarity with military life one can tell from certain passages in his writings that he most likely took part in fighting in the Ambonese region, probably on Seram, against the combined forces of Makassarese and Ambonese in what came to be known as the "Fifth Ambonese War" which lasted, according to Rumphius, from 1651 to 1656.[29]

Rumphius survived. What is more, the VOC recognized that he had more valuable talents. They sent him to appraise and repair defensive structures on several islands and used his mathematical skills for military purposes. VOC contracts were for five years. In 1657, Rumphius was permitted to resign from the military and allowed to enter the civilian branch of the VOC as a junior merchant stationed on the island of Ambon. There he remained for the rest of his life. Rumphius had been soldiering off and on for about ten years. It had been an important part of his life and proved to be a lasting influence. The self-sufficiency he had acquired would be severely tested in a series of calamities that befell him a decade later, but it also reflects a strong character that had its rough side and an indomitable will that did not conform or submit.

This self-reliant man was about to change himself into something entirely new and different. Like Camoens, Portugal's great national poet, Rumphius exchanged the sword for the pen. This transformation from unknown soldier to a representative man who is still admired took place in a region he aptly called the "Water Indies." In the preface to his *Herbal,* Rumphius told his readers: "The Water-Indies stretch from Sumatra, then Java, and the other large Islands, in a long chain to the East, once nicely called the eyelids of the world by *Julius Scaliger*, then with the South-Easter Islands they curve to the North and North-west, through the Moluccos, to end in the North with the *Phillipine* or *Manilhase* Islands. In the most remote corner of these Water-Indies to the East, one will find the three governments, of Amboina, the Moluccas, and Banda; these are enclosed in the East and separated from the South Sea by the land which one is wont to call *Nova Guinea*." Rumphius was quite correct to emphasize the presence of water because in Indonesia its area is three times greater than the land's. The Indonesians speak of their country as *Tanah Air*, land and water, almost as if one word.

Far to the east was the small island of Ambon, which despite its diminutive size — it is only 32 miles long and 10 miles wide — had been delegated a disproportionate importance due to the European determination to monopolize the spice trade. During the sixteenth century, the Portuguese made Ambon the headquarters of the Spice Islands, and the Dutch maintained that status during the seventeenth. One could compare the island to a lobster claw, with the northern peninsula like a large upper pincer, called Hitu, and the smaller lower one called Leitimor. Rumphius lived for thirteen years on the coast of Hitu, first at Larike, a small settlement in the west, then for a decade in Hila, further to the east. It might seem a lonely existence to us but it probably was not. Rumphius was his own boss. His duties were exacting but not exhausting. As long as he took care of business first, the VOC would not bother him.

Larike had about 800 inhabitants. Rumphius lived outside a small redoubt that housed a garrison of about two dozen. It was in Larike that he began to collect botanical, zoological, and mineralogical items and started to register them in the vivid prose which has survived three centuries.

To put it as briefly as possible, Rumphius composed a natural history of eastern Indonesia, modeled on Pliny's classic work. Let me immediately add that Rumphius' achievement was greater than that of the Roman cavalry officer because no matter how much one admires the Latin volumes they remain a particular reader's digest of over a hundred authorities. Rumphius' equally voluminous writings are mostly original, based on first-hand investigation and information. For all sorts of reasons, he was prevented from shaping the various parts into a single whole, but the independent components are monumental in their own right. His greatest achievement was a herbal of eastern Indonesia entitled *Het Amboinsche Kruidboek* (The Ambonese Herbal), and his most popular achievement was *D'Amboinsche Rariteitkamer* or *The Ambonese Curiosity Cabinet*, published posthumously in 1705. It discussed tropical crustaceans in book one, mollusks in book two, and minerals and sundry curiosities in book three. Its popularity was primarily due to the illustrations of shells in book two. Rumphius also wrote a geographical description and a history of Ambon. Towards the end of his life he was working on a book about Moluccan animals and he had written a dictionary of Malay, completed up to the letter "P." But Rumphius never saw any of this in print. The only things published during his lifetime were a report of the catastrophic earthquake of 1674 and thirteen brief notes about Asian natural history in a learned journal back in Germany.

He started this unbelievable amount of work in the 1650s, accomplishing all of it in about forty years, at the same time pursuing an active career in the VOC, doing most of the actual writing during the final three decades of his life. And his career was successful. When he was assigned to Hila, the second-most important post on the island, he was promoted to "merchant," a high position for a foreigner. Sometime during these years on Hitu, Rumphius probably married a woman named Susanna. They had several children, but it is not known how many. We know he had a son, Paulus Augustus (?1663–1706), who helped him later on, but it is very frustrating that there is no further information about Susanna except for her husband's brief, poignant mention in his *Herbal*. Describing an orchid variety that had no local name, he called it in Latin *Flos susannae*, and in Malay *Bonga Susanna*, "in memory of her who when alive was my first Companion and Helpmate in the gathering of herbs and plants, and who was also the first ever to show this flower to me." Whoever she was, if Susanna lived with Rumphius in Hila she shared an enjoyable existence. He had a comfortable dwelling, abundant food, and a large, armed vessel at his disposal, and the prospect from a moderate elevation was that of beautiful Piru Bay. In that era of clean air he could see the neighboring island of Seram.

During the day Rumphius took care of business, also gathered and collected, and received items from other parts of the region either on consignment or as gifts. At night he wrote. From the point of view of modern ophthalmology, lighting in Rumphius' house was an abomination. The most common light source was a dish with coconut or kenari oil, with a float of gaba marrow and a piece of cotton for a wick — charming and decorative, but rather pitiful when pitted against the eclipse of a tropic night. During the day, he spent many hours scouring the beaches. Most of them were sand deriving from pulverized shells, magnificently but cruelly white under the forbidding sun. Rumphius blamed the beaches, but I think it was a combination of both day labor and night work which caused him to lose his sight. In the preface to his *Herbal* he contends that it was field research that assassinated his vision: "From such walking in the heat of the Sun my sight was struck to such an extent by a Suffusio or Cataracta Nigra, that I lost most of it within three months." By May 9, 1670, the governor of Ambon reported to his superiors in Java that "the Merchant Rumphius became blind several weeks ago." He was forty-two years old. Today the problem would have been diagnosed as glaucoma and it can be cured, but for Rumphius it meant blindness.

The idyll at Hila was over. This man who had survived shipwreck, military service in foreign countries, sea travel, and a voluntary exile to what was quite literally the other side of the world, this survivor was now faced with the worst calamity of all. It did not destroy him, but for someone who could word a flower or a plant in the most delicate detail, it must have been devastating and one must concede that his achievement is all the more remarkable for it. A phrase from a letter to a European colleague in 1680 says it all; blindness, he wrote, "suddenly took away from me the entire world and all its creatures."[30] And misfortune was not through with him yet.

Deemed unfit to do his job, Rumphius was ordered by his immediate superior to vacate his post and move himself and his family to the only true town on the island, Kota Ambon, the capital. There, during a celebration of Chinese New Year on February 17, 1674, the entire island was hit by one of the worst tectonic earthquakes in Ambon's history. Rumphius, Susanna, and at least one daughter were strolling down a street in the Chinese quarter. A contemporary eyewitness reported that Rumphius' wife and daughter were "called over by a certain Chinese woman and invited in, now when they felt the first shaking they wanted to walk away, but instead they got the wall of the house on their backs, and thus lamentably suffocated beneath it, notwithstanding that they were dug up as soon as was possible. Just before that time Rumphius had gone for an evening stroll past the very same house and had even been called over by his wife and daughter, but he demurred; which shows that God was disposed to keep him from harm, for if he had sat down, there is no doubt that there would have been no escape for him, due to his blindness. It was a piteous sight to see that man sit next to his corpses, and also to hear his lamentations, concerning both this accident and his blindness."[31]

Fate considered even this loss not quite sufficient yet. First his vision had been taken from him, then Susanna, now his writing became a target. The VOC froze him in the rank of "merchant" and used him as what we would call a consultant.

In other words, he lived at the behest of the Company and could work only by the mercy of substitute eyes and pens. I am convinced that his writing sheltered him from despair, but he needed help. To its credit, the Company provided him with amanuenses to take down his dictation and draughtsmen to produce the illustrations he used to draw himself. One has to realize that after 1670, his blindness forced him to start writing his *Herbal* all over again. As was customary during that century, he had first written it in Latin, but there were not many people in the Indies who could take down Latin dictation, so he was forced to switch to the language of his mother's family. Yet there were benefits. The rewrite imposed by this practical need also gave him the chance to produce a vernacular text that would be of practical use to the common man. As he announced in the preface to the *Herbal*, it was addressed "particularly to those who live in the Indies" because those people could use it as a medical vade mecum. And this was perfectly reasonable; many of his European contemporaries preferred the herbal medicine of the Indonesian *dukuns* (healers) to the bloody incompetence of Western physicians. Rumphius' herbal is in that respect a huge materia medica, a repository of herbal knowledge and remedies that is of great value to ethnographers and ethnobotanists. And, finally, the enforced switch to Dutch also produced a far more expressive and original prose than the constraints of Latin composition had permitted.

Though the text had to be entirely rewritten, he had at least all the illustrations, in color, which he had finished himself before 1670. But all these priceless images, along with manuscripts and all his books, were reduced to ashes in 1687 during a major fire that raged through the European quarter of Kota Ambon. Rumphius' house burned down to the ground. About a decade later someone stole 61 new illustrations from his study. But he persisted. In 1680 he had half of his huge herbal finished once again. It was shipped to Java where the manuscript was going to be consigned to a ship that was part of that year's retour fleet to Holland. Thanks to his curiosity and to the peremptory powers of his office, however, the reigning governor general, by the name of Joannes Camphuys (1634–1695), ordered his clerks to copy Rumphius' text because, as an ardent naturalist, he wanted it for his private enjoyment. Camphuys' authoritarian dictate proved to be a saving grace. It took time to copy all those pages, and not until two years later did the first six books of the *Ambonese Herbal* set sail for Holland. But Holland and England were locked in a war with France's Sun King, and Rumphius' manuscript became an innocent victim. A French naval squadron attacked the retour fleet and sank the ship that bore those hard-won pages.

Once again, Rumphius rallied. He even took the opportunity to make additions and corrections to the now only existing copy of the first six books, the one Camphuys had ordered. The other six reconstituted and copied books of the *Herbal* made it across the ocean without incident, and by 1697, only five years before his death, the entire work was safely in Holland, though it would not be in print until more than half a century had passed. During his final years Rumphius also completed the *Ambonese Curiosity Cabinet* and several other works. He kept on adding to the herbal until by 1701 he had what amounted to another, supplementary volume, which was dispatched to Holland in 1701, only nine months before his death.

The very last chapter of this supplementary volume contains a description of the Javanese mongoose. This seems a peculiar conclusion to a work about plants, but Rumphius was fond of this animal and wanted his readers to know about it, and since, as he wrote at the beginning of the chapter, he "doubted that [his] weakness and old age would permit him to finish the book on Native Animals" he was working on, he added this final chapter as an insurance against oblivion. It is a charming sketch that in modesty and affection for a fellow creature provides a quiet but telling farewell to a remarkable life. Since Rumphius lived in the tropics it was only natural that he extolled the animal's prowess as a snake killer, but the real emphasis is on the shape, quickness, and engaging temperament of the "Moncus" (as he called the *Herpestes javanicus*, a member of the Civet-cat genus). This Indonesian ancestor of Kipling's Rikki-Tikki-Tavi is consumed with curiosity, a character trait that it shared with its aging master. "This Animal is incredibly quick, when it stands or sits upright, the head is never still for a moment, and it inspects everything that passes, be it people or animals." Perhaps the animal's affectionate nature was more important to an old man with little companionship. "But it is even more amazing how tame this Animal becomes, and how used it gets to the people who keep it company. It is difficult to grab hold of by its back, since it will immediately slip out of your hands if you grab it like that, yet you can touch it with your hands from the front, and it will presently seize them, and do the same with the legs of whoever walks by. In short, it becomes so tame that it even sleeps with people." Rumphius captured the Moncus with one of the characteristic metaphoric images which carry his work beyond the scientific imperative. He says that it will take hold of whatever one gives it to eat with its two front paws, which, "when it has nothing to do, it puts on its chest, like a poor sinner."

Rumphius died on June 15, 1702, at the age of seventy-four. He was buried in a plot outside Kota Ambon, and an unknown admirer erected a modest marble tomb in his honor. During the British interregnum, the British governor of Ambon destroyed the grave site and sold the marble for profit. The grave was restored by the Dutch government and a discreet monument dedicated to the naturalist's memory in 1824. That memorial was also destroyed, this time during an allied bombing raid in the Second World War. In 1996, a third monument was dedicated in downtown Kota Ambon, but its fate is also in jeopardy due to the sectarian and religious war that has been raging in that region since 1999, and that has cost the lives of 4,000 people and forced half a million other victims to become refugees.

The volume at hand presents all the descriptions of orchids that Rumphius included in his monumental herbal, *Het Amboinsche Kruidboek* (The Ambonese Herbal). It was written between 1657 and 1697 and is, therefore, a *seventeenth*-century text. It was published (at a minimum) half a century later: in six volumes, plus an addition or seventh volume, between 1741 and

1755, which makes some people mistakenly believe that it was a eighteenth-century text.

The first half of the complete title translates as: "The Ambonese Herbal, Being a Description of the most noteworthy Trees, Shrubs, Herbs, Land- and Water-Plants, which are found in Amboina, and the surrounding Islands, According to their shape, various names, cultivations, and use: together with several insects and animals. For the most part with the Figures pertaining to them. All gathered with much trouble and diligence over many years, and described in twelve books by Georgius Everhardus Rumphius."[32]

The seven volumes contain 1,661 folio pages, divided into twelve "books," 876 chapters, that are illustrated with 696 plates. As the titles of the individual books indicated, the Rumphian divisions are unlike those of modern botanical practice. Book one describes trees "that bear edible Fruits, and that are planted by People in their Gardens": book two contains the "Spice Trees": book three describes those trees that "produce some Resin, notable Flowers or hurtful Milk": book four presents "wild Trees, that are turned into Lumber"; book five, a mixture of wild trees; book six presents wild and cultivated shrubs; book seven, "Forest-ropes," which are lianas, as well as "creeping Shrubs"; book eight describes the all-important "Garden plants that serve as food, Medicine, or recreation"; book nine "twining Plants"; book ten presents a medley of "Wild Herbs"; book eleven deals with the remaining "wild Herbs"; and book twelve describes "the Sea-trees, and stony Marine growths, that resemble a Plant," that is to say coral and algae. The *Auctuarium,* or "volume seven," has additions to any of the above categories. Merrill has estimated that Rumphius' *Amboinsche Kruidboek* describes about 1,700 floral forms.[33]

There is order to Rumphius' method. Each plant is first described in graphic and often poetic detail. Rumphius is one of the greatest phytographers in the history of botany, and unsurpassed as the phytographer of tropical flora. After the description, the plant's names are given. First is the Latin one which, more often than not, was an original label with Rumphius as its author. Next comes the indigenous Malay name, if any, and thereafter whichever other Indonesian names Rumphius might have heard. Other Indonesian names often included are Ambonese ones, even distinguishing what a plant is called on the northern peninsula (Hitu) of the island or on southern Leitimor; Macassarese names are frequently provided, as are Javanese and Balinese appellations; also frequent are names from Ternate, nearby islands (such as Buru, Seram, the Banda islands), other Moluccan islands, New Guinea, and so on. Rumphius frequently provides Chinese cognomens, more specifically, names from southern coastal China. And every nominative section provides, of course, a Dutch simile, almost always original, descriptive, and memorable.

Even by the standards of modern scientific taxonomy, Rumphius' *Herbal* is very important because, as Merrill points out, "its descriptions and figures typify a very large number of binomials of later authors."[34] Merrill's final judgment is that "as an original source the Herbarium Amboinense stands preëminent among all the early publications on Malayan botany. In more than 800 original 'publications' of species of plants under the binomial system from 1753 to 1908 the Rumphian names or figures, or both, are quoted as synonyms, and in about 350 cases the proposed binomials are based wholly on data given by Rumphius."[35]

After naming names come place and provenance. The above sketch of Rumphian nomenclature makes it abundantly clear that, though the title of his herbal sounds restrictive, he really cast his botanical net far and wide. Rumphius refers to plants from Java, Celebes (Sulawesi), Ceram (Seram), Bali, the Banda islands, Buru, the true Moluccas (Ternate, Tidore, Bacian, Halmahera, the latter also known as Gilolo), the Sumbawa-Timor group of islands (Nusa Tenggara), the Philippines, Manipa, Buton, Borneo, Sumatra, the Sula islands, Ambon's small neighboring islands, the Aru islands, New Guinea, and the Kei islands, as well as making frequent references to countries beyond Indonesia, such as China, Japan, Indo-China, Malacca, Madagascar, South Africa, Mexico, Peru, and Brazil.

After description, name, and place, a chapter's concluding discussion is of the plant's use. This section was very important at the time: one of Rumphius' main objectives was to provide a medical vade mecum for Europeans living in Indonesia. Even if a plant has no medicinal significance, Rumphius will always mention whatever economic use of which he had become aware. In other words, he provides scholars of our era with a volumi-nous text of ethnobotany. Natural products had to satisfy every human need in his preindustrial era, from construction materials to writing implements. The range of his information is astonishing. It includes recipes (for instance, for a mussel sauce), food habits, fashion information, natural writing utensils, how to black shields and forge swords, remedies against conception, remedies to promote conception, how to cleanse the digestive system of the newborn, how to ward off the troubled sleep of children by placing certain shells under their pillows, and so on. He includes stories, folklore, religious practices—in short things both marvelous and quotidian. All of this and more is overlooked if one is satisfied with a mere index of his plants and animals. This sympathetic appropriation of a different reality was an act of enthusiasm, and students of Indonesian ethnography can only thank fate that Rumphius was a pre-modern animist because a Cartesian would have scoffed at and dismissed most of what he recorded. An example from the present orchid texts is the Alfuran warriors who stuck *Dendrobium* blooms behind their glass armbands before they went out to gather severed heads.

Besides the ethnobotanical dimension of the *Herbal*, the other strikingly modern feature of this classic text is Rumphius' working methods. Like a good scientist he based his text on nearly thirteen years (from 1657 to 1670) of personal field observations, use of local informants, and a professional correspondence with natural historians in other parts of the VOC's farflung empire. He maintained the latter two channels for nearly half a century. Like any good modern anthropologist, but very rare in the seventeenth century, Rumphius cultivated the friendship of informants. What makes this even more as-

Courtesy of Theo Laurentius. From the Collection Laurentius.

tonishing is that he acknowledged their help, an act of grati-
tude that was very uncommon at the time, especially in the
colonies. He will call them "Master," mention them by name,
and state that it is "only decent to commemorate" (2:241) their
instruction.

We know that he made field observations, not only from
such statements as "I measured everything the way I saw it in
these Islands" (5:126), but also from the only other known portrait besides the one his son, Paulus, drew of his father, which
is reprinted here as the frontispiece. In that portrait Rumphius
is standing in a tropical forest, observing a workman climbing a ficus tree while writing down his observations in a *tafelet*
(from the Italian *tavolette*, called *papier à tablette* in French). An
art historian discovered these sketchbooks for artists, but he
also mentioned that similar booklets were given by the VOC
to its employees.[36] The writing implement, kept in two loops
that were attached to the tafelet, was a metalpoint stylus (see
above). The pages in the booklets were reusable and "the advan-

Courtesy of Leiden University Library.

tage of the use of metalpoint over drawing or writing materials like chalk or ink is that it does not smudge, it is 'dry,' and it leaves a very fine and controlled line. That is the reason why it was used for very detailed drawings."[37] This was obviously an ideal tool in a tropical environment. Above Rumphius is seen holding one in this rare image of him as a working botanist.

Despite all superficial appearances, Rumphius' botanical examinations are closer to an Asian than a European system of knowledge. His nomenclature was based on original Indonesian nomination, and his ethnobotany is almost purely Indonesian. He was well aware of this. He warned people not to assume that an apparent similarity between an Indonesian and a European plant meant they were identical: "when one examines and judges an unknown plant, one should not be too astonished by the shape and resemblance to our European plants, but one should first inquire about its nature among the Natives" (6:178). In the preface to the *Herbal* he insists that he "knowingly" included odd local facts, which Westerners might dismiss as foolish fables or dangerous superstitions, "not because I have absolute faith in them, or because I want to force the Reader to believe them, but because among those fables one will always find some truth and some of nature's hidden qualities. . . ." The greater number of the plants he was describing and gathering, including the orchids, were unknown and alien to Europe. When he read a Western book, it sometimes must have seemed printed in an unaccustomed tongue. In fact, because his mind and training were pre-modern and pre-Linnean, he was more receptive to the Asian reality that surrounded him.

Rumphius introduced a multitude of new plants to the Old World. His work is replete with original observations and botanical firsts, and his presentation of tropical orchids is no exception. He described the orchids in fifteen chapters in book eleven (chs. 1 through 15), one (ch. 70) from book eight, and one (ch. 64) from book ten.

Rumphius was the first botanist to describe epiphytes and to intuit that these plants were not parasites but that their arboreal hosts were only something of a perch. He was the first to *describe* orchid seed (he even uses the actual word "seed," which is *zaad* in Dutch, see 6:110, 115) and seems to have comprehended that orchid seeds are dispersed by the wind. He also clearly understood orchid fruits and was the first to note the presence of pollinia, which have been defined as "more or less coherent mass[es] of pollen."[38] The first chapter includes the first known description of a "trash basket"—a particular structure with which certain orchid species gather essential nourishment—and the first mention of myrmecophytic orchids, which are orchids that have ants living in a symbiotic relationship in their pseudobulbs. To Conrad Gessner (1516–1565) goes the honor of having been the first to *draw* orchid seed (from *Elleborine amplexicaulis multiflora*). His rendition was printed in his *Opera Botanica*, which appeared posthumously between 1751 and 1771, that is, *after* Rumphius' work was published, since volume six, which contains Rumphius' orchid texts, was printed in 1750, though the descriptions were written prior to 1697.[39] His correct assumption about orchid seed and pollinia contributed to Rumphius' dismissal of the then prevalent myths of how these plants propagated,[40] anticipating modern knowledge. Several times he mentions floral remnants on fruits, and he appears to be the first botanist to have noted this common post-pollination phenomenon.

Rumphius was also "the first to find and describe any member of the genus *Phalaenopsis*."[41] The species he introduced was *Phalaenopsis amabilis*, described in the second chapter, an orchid which by happy coincidence was selected as Indonesia's national flower.[42] By another fortuitous act of serendipity it was the nineteenth-century botanist Carl Ludwig Blume (1796–1862) who rediscovered this same species and in 1825, nearly a century and a half after Rumphius' original discovery, established the genus of these epiphytic monopodials, calling it *Phalaenopsis*.[43] Only about 40 species of *Phalaenopsis* are known, and many of these are threatened by extinction.[44] The Blume connection is serendipitous because, like Rumphius, he was born a German (from Brunswick), went to the Dutch colonial Indies as a botanist at the age of twenty-two, and lived on Java from 1818 to 1826; thereafter he became the director of the National Herbarium in Leiden.

The 36 orchid species, plus 12 uncertified ones (counts will vary), presented in this book are the first Indonesian orchids described by anyone. Rumphius is the founder of Indonesian botanical exploration, the father of Indonesian orchidology, and one of the earliest pioneers of Asian botany. He still speaks to us across three centuries because of his gifts as a prose writer. Rumphius' descriptions are lively and lifelike. The prose is animated, it is embodied prose. It is a rueful irony that Rumphius' blindness forced him to marshal the two more intimate senses of touch and taste. For him four senses became tropes of understanding that render these living denizens of the tropics as if perceived for the first time.

For the European of the seventeenth century, the Moluccas were a far and distant prospect, but Rumphius believed it could be disclosed by means of language. In essence he wrote with the mission of a poet, using the familiar to illustrate the strange. Thus the keyboard of a clavichord is used in his description of a cluster of bananas, a mizzen sail describes a jellyfish, and in his description of how the Chinese use the operculum of mollusks for incense, he compared that use to "a Basse in Musick which, when heard alone has no comeliness, but which when mixed with other voices, makes for a sweet accord." Metaphors illustrate. Note that the two elements of the trope have not changed: a bass is still the lower half of the tonal range, and an operculum is still the animal's cover to close off its shell after it has retracted. But each element is enriched when the two are brought together by the imagination.

The example of Rumphius intimates the possibility that science and poetry can be conciliated, that an act of will and the legislation of the imagination can turn remote facts into familiar poetry. Rumphius accomplished this for his readers then and still does for us today, because the elegant simplicity of his prose is the perfect response to his and our experience of the natural world. As a modern botanist once wrote: "Rumphius showed the way and set the standards."[45]

ABOUT THIS TRANSLATION

Rumphius wrote his *Herbal* between 1657 and 1697, hence the text translated here is from the second half of the seventeenth century and has nothing in common with practices of the mid-eighteenth century, which is the time when it was finally published. I have tried to engender a smoothly readable text that is as close to seventeenth-century English as possible. I did not include any vocabulary that was not current during the seventeenth century, nor do these pages conform to our standardized publishing practices. The reason for the latter is twofold. First, one has to keep in mind that the manuscript the printer used was not Rumphius' original work. That is lost forever. What the printer used was a copied copy. On top of that, the pages Rumphius rewrote, after his original work sank beneath the waves, were *dictated.* Since he was blind by that time he could not check the accuracy of the transcription, with the result that the text is rife with bizarre spellings and other oddities. I left them. It is pointless to second-guess Rumphius' intentions, and I see no need to do so.

The second reason for strange locutions is that what was already a compromised text was then once more jeopardized by the rather lax practices of eighteenth-century printers (who were also the publishers of their time). For one thing, editors were unknown, a state of things to which we seem to have returned. Rumphius was well aware of these pitfalls and in the preface warned his readers that the *Herbal* "will contain many misbegotten words, and bad spellings of strange words, as will be the case with all such works that are realized with borrowed eyes and hands." Since I refuse to commit a modern paring of the genuine article, I have kept all its idiosyncrasies: the particular nomenclature, the peculiar spelling, the unfamiliar punctuation, and the lapses where the printer simply left things out.

I have tried to present Rumphius to you, not a modern approximation. We have no right to interpose a modern voice. If we merely want to extract certain information from classic texts such as this one, then we should be satisfied with epitomes, and there are several in existence. They just need to be updated. There is no reason why someone cannot produce a readable translation without our (usually ugly) jargon. Some have urged me to ignore the integrity of the translator's task and substitute familiar modern nomenclature for the colorful original. I prefer not to.

Rumphius' work is pre-Linnean; the Swedish scientist was born five years after Rumphius died, hence the Dutch-German botanist never knew the terminology that Linnaeus imposed on the scientific world from about the middle of the eighteenth century. For instance, Linnaeus used the Latin noun *pollen* (which means "fine flour" or "fine dust") for the first time in 1751 (in *Philosophia botanica*), nearly half a century after Rumphius was buried on Ambon. It would be incongruous to use "pollen" when Rumphius uses "meal" for the powdery substance the anther discharges. I had no problem resisting such calls of expediency over artistic integrity because I wanted to give my readers Rumphius, not a bloodless digest.

It is difficult to translate a work that was written in seventeenth-century Dutch and that dealt with so many different subjects—botany, history, linguistics, ethnographic detail, medical advice, and much more. I have tried to explicate as much as possible in my annotations, which incorporate information from a number of specialists. The usual caveat prevails: what is printed is my responsibility. For those interested in the primary tools employed in rendering this English version, I relied, first of all, on the large Dutch dictionary *Het Woordenboek der Nederlandsche Taal*. Based on historical principles, its twenty-nine volumes were published between 1864 and 1998 and reputedly constitute the largest single-language dictionary in the world. For English I perused primarily the *Oxford English Dictionary* because its wordhoard was more relevant than American English, since the latter did not exist in Rumphius' day. Practical help is available in *Een glossarium van zeventiende-eeuws Nederlands*, compiled by P. G. J. van Sterkenburg, while of much more modest benefit was William Sewel's *A New Dictionary English and Dutch*, published in 1691.

None of these orchid texts were ever translated into English before.

RUMPHIUS' ORCHIDS

Chapter One

THE INSCRIBED ANGREK.

We shall now describe the Aristocrats of wild plants, who convey their nobility by wanting to live only high up in trees, and never below on the ground, just as one will commonly see Noble Castles and Fortresses built on high, wherefore they have a strange way of growing and are strangely fashioned, just like Aristocrats flaunting their finery. The Moluccan Princesses add a third reason, to wit, that they will not permit anyone to wear these flowers unless they be Gentle Ladies. But one will also find among these Nobles some who, as is the case with people, will change into Peasants, and grow on the ground, and these seem to form a particular family.[1] Wherefore I must divide all Angreks into two main classes:

I. Into the Aristocracy, which will grow only on trees, and secondly, into the Peasantry, which grows on the ground, yet all are related to the plant, that is called *Helleborine*[2] or *Calceolus mariae*[3] in the Herbals, and which is divided into so many kinds, that I will not be able to describe them all.[4] But I have comprehended the Aristocracy under the following twelve kinds, of which the first and most beautiful is *Angraecum scriptum*,[5] described in this Chapter.

Angraecum scriptum is a rare plant, that grows on trees like Mistletoe,[6] where it appears on the thickest branches, mostly at their base, or from the joints,[7] with countless tough, white fibers, attaching themselves to the selfsame bark, and it has many white points, upright, as on a Hedgehog, but not prickly.

From this issue some large, rather flat, cone-shaped purses, divided transversely into joints, with deep furrows or stripes lengthwise, with an inner substance that is plant-like and slimy, wherefrom sprout three or four long and narrow leaves, that embrace one another, like those of the white *Hellebore*, or *Hyris*,[8] thick, stiff, narrow in back, then gradually broadening, easily a foot long, three fingers[9] wide, traversed[10] lengthwise by three sinews, that do not bulge very much, though the central one forms a groove[11] on the inside; another stem comes from the root next to this purse, round, without leaves, four to five feet long, somewhat curved at the top, whereon the flowers grow orderly above each other, in the manner of Hyacinths. Each one on its separate bandy little stem.

Now these flowers have a particular shape, and would like to resemble those called *Satyrium*,[12] the size of a narcissus, fashioned from five outer leaflets, narrow in back, wide in front, some yellow, some a yellowish green, whereon one will see broad drops or characters, as if Hebrew letters,[13] but not distinctly so, all of them a brownish red, different on each flower.

In the center is another hollow leaflet, rolled inwards, like a tiny beaker, of a lighter color, with brown or purple stripes, and in this hollow one will see a thick little pillar, with a broad little head; otherwise it lacks scent.

The first flower that opens up is yellow-green inside, and its characters are a dark brown, but in time it turns a true yellow, and its characters become red; it lives for a long time, even on stems that have been broken off, for, when put in a room, they will bear flowers for as long as eight days, opening up one after another. And they finally begin to wither, but without falling off, and their feet become thick and bellied, and form the fruit, which resembles a young *Blimbing*,[14] or a six-sided, fat pod, and the edges have bulging ridges, of which the three bigger ones are furrowed, and are split in two towards the front; the other three are lower, and not furrowed. It is five inches long, one and a half inch thick, widest in front, with the withered flower on top, more pointed in back, with a green, thick, plant-like bark on the outside, while the inside is filled with a yellow, downy meal.

The ripe ones turn a dark gray, split easily into six parts, in such a way that the ridges in back and in front remain attached to each other, like an Imperial crown,[15] and then most of the yellow [meal] falls out and is scattered[16] on the wind, but it is still unknown whether it contains a seminal power, enabling it to transplant itself when the wind has borne it to other trees.[17]

As I mentioned, the purses, which bear the leaves, are plant-like inside, but when the leaves have fallen off, they become thicker, and finally dry up, with a substance inside that is spongy and fibrous, and that usually has ants nestled inside.

There are some variations of the foregoing, but none of them are different enough to make for a separate kind. Firstly, the plants that grow on Mangas[18] or suchlike trees, with sappy bark, have larger leaves than the preceding one, to wit, twenty-seven or eight inches long, easily the width of a hand,[19] with no other notable sinew down its length except for the central one, instead of three, as the foregoing has, and they resemble the young leaves of the Spatwortel [Dart Root].[20]

I once had a flower-bearing stem that was five and a half feet long, with some bows that had fifty-two blooms on them at the same time. Its characters did not resemble Hebrew so much, as old Latin Capitals,[21] and some looked like Samaritan letters[22] as well, wherewith one would be able to make up some names, if one took a leaf of a flower here and there, and laid them out in some sort of order.

If a branch of the Mangas tree, whereon the Angreck and similar herbs are planted, were to provide food for them, it will not bear any fruit, or very little, which one should endure for the sake of a handsome show.

There is another variation on the Kalappus tree, which many consider a particular kind, so I will describe it in detail. It grows on the sides of old Kalappus trees; the root forms a hillock or large clump of fine, long, though not prickly points. The purses are similar to the foregoing, but smooth, without demarcations or joints, except that it is slightly ribbed lengthwise. The leaves are somewhat shorter, wider, and thicker, without any sinews, except for the central groove, thirteen to sixteen inches long, four wide, and appear on the young purses. The flower stem has a peculiar appearance, five to six and a half feet long, as thick as one's little finger, round, stiff, and almost woody. The two top thirds are covered with flowers, not unlike the foregoing, to wit, fashioned from five yellow-green leaves, of which one is always curved inwards, and almost every flower has a little curve at its origin, usually curving upwards, some sideways.

These leaflets are decorated with coarse, brown characters, which one cannot say are specific shapes, for most of them resemble spots, though one could discern [the shape of the letters] A. J. O. among them. There is a little chalice in the center, slightly paler than the outer leaves, with brown lines down the length of it, otherwise scentless.

The fruits are undoubtedly large, angular pods, similar to the foregoing. The clump of roots would almost provide a load for a man. It blooms in November.

The Balinese do not have a special name for it, though they will not recognize it as *Angrec kringsing*, wherefore I have named it tentatively *Angrec calappa*,[23] since it is found near the crown of such a tree; others call it *Angrec lida*,[24] because of the smooth and stiff leaves, which resemble a large tongue.

Name. In Latin *Angraecum scriptum* or *Helleborine Mollucca*; In Malay *Angrek* or *Bonga Boki* and *Bonga putri*;[25] on Ternate *Saja baki*, that is to say *Flos principissae*, for reasons given above. Others call it *Saja ngawa* or *Ngawan*; In Balinese *Angrec kringsing*, because the flowers are painted like a certain kind of cloth called *Kringsing*.[26]

All these flowers are called *Rangrec*[27] in Javanese; the Portuguese call them *Fulha alacra* or *Fulha lacre*.[28] However, that is really a particular kind on Java, that smells like Musk, and is called such because the flower and its tail look like a Scorpion.

Some Malay also call all *Angrecs*, *Api api*,[29] since they share the opinion that they come forth from the seed, or the waste of certain Birds, blaming this particularity on the little *Cacopit*[30] bird, a kind of *Regulus,* though this is not very likely, since this little Bird does not frequent Mangi-mangi trees[31] much, but goes instead to shrubs that have flowers, wherefrom it sucks the sap or dew, but it has the name for seeding all mistletoe with its waste.[32]

Place. It only grows on thick branches of trees in the wild and in the mountains, on Kanari trees[33] as well as on varieties of Mangi-mangi trees on the beach, and is known throughout these Eastern Islands. If one lifts it gently with all its roots, one can transplant it to a Mangas tree near a house, after having smeared a little mud on the branches first, and tying it down with a string, and it will produce flowers every year, though they will never have that beautiful yellow of those that grow in the wild.[34]

I have often tried to plant it in garden soil, but it only produced leaves, and I have never been able to make it produce flowers, though they were there for many years; afterward I found a half-rotted log in the forest that they grew on, brought it home, and put it deep into the ground, and the Angrek did grow and bloom on it, but when the log finally fell apart, the plant expired as well.[35]

Remains only to determine if it can be preserved when one cuts off an entire green branch and buries it in the ground at an angle. Otherwise we will have to be satisfied, that nature allows us to feed this beautiful show on our neighboring Mangas trees.

It is difficult to guess how these plants get on the trees in the wild. It is pointless to believe that they grow from the dirt on the bark, as Moss does and Ferns, for then they should have different shapes on totally different trees, nor would one be able to transplant them just like that, but if one notices that, as it were, they were placed on it, even on smooth barks, like that of Kanari trees,[36] it is more likely, that they are either seeded from their own seed by the wind, or by the birds, as, for instance, Waringin trees,[37] and all sorts of Viscum.[38]

One might be able to posit, that the true seminal power resides in some kernels the size of a Catjang,[39] which are sometimes found in the aforementioned yellow meal of the fruits, though they be rather watery. Similar kernels, bigger than others, in the fruits of various Waringas, are also thought to be seed kernels.

Use. The only use of these flowers is to be a delight for the eyes, after one cuts them off with the entire stem, and puts them for a few days in a room, not in water, but naked on a clump of soil, for if this plant gets into water, it will stink like dishwater, or like most kinds of Orchis, and the fresh sap smells like that as well. The great Ladies of Ternate, particularly the wives, sisters, and daughters of their Kings (which are all called *Putri* in Malay or *Buki* in the Moluccas), reserve these flowers for themselves, and they would put a great affront upon a common woman, not to mention a female Slave, if they were to wear this flower on their head. Wherefore they have these flowers brought from the forest only for them, so they can wear them in their hair, reasoning that nature itself indicates that these flowers are not suitable for ordinary people, because they grow only in high places, which is why it has the aforementioned name.

If someone is suffering from whitlow,[40] he should take the plant-like marrow of the purse, crush it with some Curcuma[41] in salt water, and tie it around the finger, which will make the sore quickly ripen, while it even goes away sometimes, if it has not quite set yet.

If one takes the peeled purses, and mash the inner marrow with a little Ginger, and then smear it on the stomach, it will itch a little at first, but not for long, whereafter it will kill worms, and immediately expel all bad humours from the intestines; indeed, it will even shrink a swollen Spleen or *Tehatu*, and the same is tied to swollen legs, to draw out the dropsy.

If one chews the marrow of the bulbs, until the sap comes out, and then rinses one's mouth with it, it will drive out thrush, because it is tasteless and strongly cooling.

The Ambonese have a secret, though superstitious way, to make a Philter from the fruit's yellow meal, saying that a Woman will pursue that person who puts it in her food or drink. It is otherwise indeed taken with food, to stop the Bloody Flux, and is quite tasteless.

I called it *Helleborine Molucca*, because it resembles *Helleborine recentiorum* the most, which *Clusius*[42] describes in *Lib. 2. rar. Plant. Cap. 63.*,[43] while it is also called *Calceolus Mariae*, and described by *Dodonaeus Lib. 6. Cap. 22.*,[44] which, according to *Gesneri,*[45] would correspond to the *Cosmosandalos*[46] of *Pausanias,*[47] or the *Chiliodynamis*[48] of the Ancients, for our *Angrec* agrees with it in the shape of its leaves, and flowers, but not in the manner of its growth. One should also examine if it bears any resemblance to the *Flos tigridis*,[49] a West-Indian flower, that *Dodon.* describes in his Latin *Appendix cap. 32.*[50]

Hieronymus Tragus[51] thinks that *Orchides* and *Satyria* develop from the seed of thrushes and blackbirds, because their excrement can sometimes be found in Fields and Pastures, where these Birds couple in Springtime.

Athanasius Kircherus' opinion in his *Mundo Subterraneo Lib. 12. Sect. 1. Cap. 9.*[52] is, that all Satyria originate either from the rotten corpses of some Animals, that still contain some seminal power, or from the seed itself of Animals that disported themselves on Mountains or in Meadows, and this can be proven by the shape [of the markings] on the flowers of the Satyria, that is either of the animal from whose seed, after it rotted in the ground, the Satyrium sprang forth, or from the insect, that commonly grows from the corpse of any Animal.[53]

One could with some reason think of our *Angrek* as well, since it shows a great kinship to *Satyrium,* that it has its origins in the seeds [dropped by] the Wild Doves, which congregate in great numbers on *Mangi-mangi* and *Kanari* trees. One might also conjecture that Pliny's *Coagulum*[54] and Gesner's *Orobanche*[55] are relatives of our *Angrec.*

Joh. Bauhinus,[56] in *Lib. 7. Cap. 3.* describes a *Viscum Indicum,*[57] which I also would guess to be some kind of *Angrec.*

The Forty Second Plate.

Shows the *enscripted* or *pyed Angrec,* growing on the trunk[58] of a *Calappus tree,* where let. A. is the bud of an *unopened flower.* B. is the *open flower,* seen from the *side,* C. is the *open flower* from *the*

Tab. XLII.

front, natural size. D. is the *Fruit.* E. the *Root* of this *plant,* grown onto a *Calappus tree.*

Comment.[59]

This Angrec corresponds to the Ansjeli Maravara in the *H. Malab. part. 12. Tab. I.,*[60] which was called by *Commel.*[61] the degenerate, juicy, Malabaran Orchis, with an odiferous and pyed flower, resembling a little bird inside,[62] also in *Fl. Malab. p. 49.*[63]

Also included here is the Viscum, with a white-spotted flower, as if a Larkspur, with a fibrous root, in *Sloan. Cat. pl. Jam. p. 120.*[64] and the *Histor. vol. I. Tab. 148. fig. 2.*[65]

Chapter Two

THE WHITE, DOUBLE ANGREK.

The second and third species of Angrek are white, consisting of a large and a small one, both with markedly different flowers from the foregoing.

I. *Angraecum album majus*[1] is almost the same plant since, first of all, it girdles[2] the trunks of trees with many long roots, a dirty white on the outside, green on the inside, with a tough sinew, that forms an entangled[3] clump under the plants, which hangs loose sometimes, and which is rougher[4] than I have seen in any other plant; the leaves are also gathered in small bunches of three or four, without purses, except for the lower stem, which is somewhat bellied, or striped.

The outer and largest leaf is between twelve and sixteen inches long, three or four fingers wide, also thick, and stiff, well-nigh without sinews, except for a groove in the center, rounded in front, and if one examines it carefully, one will note that the foremost tip is always split in two, whereof one corner is always longer than the other, which is a characteristic of all Angreks. Though it is not so apparent in the first kind, it can be clearly seen in all subsequent ones; a specific stem arises from the entangled clump of roots next to the leaves, with dark-brown lines,[5] the thickness of a quill, round, woody, and also without leaves, and it divides into a few side branches at the top, all with broad joints, from the extremity of which the flowers come forth, far fewer in number, but larger than the first kind; they also have a strange shape, which is hard to describe, and even more difficult to depict, but they grow alternately above one another, each one on its own particular white foot.

The flower is fashioned from five outer leaves, limp, pure white, of which the two on the sides are the largest; within [these five] one will see three, also white leaflets congregated, shaped like a Conch, or looking somewhat like a little Shoe, because the two lower ones curve together into a circle.

The upper leaflet stands up straighter, and has two beards at its end, that are curled up like Moustaches. In the center of this circle one will note another thick leaflet, that is divided into two tiny heads like a small pillar, colored yellow or purple, and this circle is not quite in the center of the flower, but leans towards one side. Right in the center of the flower is a tiny white hillock, from which the circle emerges, and one will find two yellow grains inside, as if these were seeds.

These yellow kernels shine through that white little hillock as if they were two eyes, and look like the head of a Grasshopper; otherwise it has no scent.

The fruit is a roundish, striped pod, easily three inches long, the thickness of a finger, with six protruding ridges, but some of these fruits have three rather than six sides, and also split open into three parts, each an inch wide, hanging together at the tip. The inner meal is a pale yellow, and falls out, but some

Tab. XLIII.

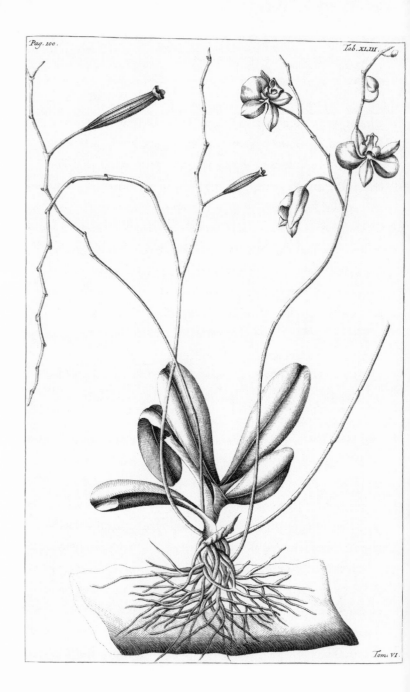

white grains remain hanging from the side threads, and if one presses them, water comes out. One will find them in October and subsequent months. This kind does have a variation, with the flower the same shape, white inside but a shiny light purple on the outside.[6] Yet another variation[7] has a flower fashioned from five extended leaflets, whereof the two on the sides are very wide, totally white, except for the inner little hillock, which is yellow.

Name. In Latin *Angraecum album majus;*[8] in Malay, *Angrec Puti besaar;* or *Bombo terbang;*[9] in Dutch *Vliegende Duive* [Flying Dove]; in Balinese *Angrec colan;* that is the *male;* because they think it is the female, the Ambonese have no name for it, but it is called *Wanlecu* on Luhu.[10]

Place. It also grows on thick but short trees, which are mossy, such as Kinar[11] and Manga[12] trees, which it climbs like a rope,[13] quite entangled, without any known use.

II. *Angraecum album minus*[14] also has stems, four or five feet long, whereof many come from one root, which is mossy, and sticks to old trees like a plaster, entwining it with many fibers.

The bottom of the stem is divided several times, first a small piece of about two inches long, the thickness of a quill, followed by a belly that is three or four inches long, the thickness of a finger, with eight ridges striped lengthwise, and transversely with three or two joints, where this belly is always a little thinner, brownish on the outside. Then the stem becomes thin again, and round, the same number of inches long, thereafter the leaves, in alternate rows over against each other, and without stems, very thick and stiff, four inches long, one and a half wide, somewhat split at the uppermost little point, and with a dark groove in the center, but the upper ones are smaller by half, with a tart taste.

The remaining stem, two foot long, is bare, and divided into dark joints, and divided at its tip into two or three other little stems, each of which bears only two or three flowers, that are much smaller than those of the foregoing, at first completely white, thereafter they become yellowish, fashioned from five leaflets, of which four are extended on one side; the fifth one is on the other side, and forms the little helmet, with two flaps, that are curved inwards like a little chalice; its upper edges are pleated,[15] and bend outwards. It too is white on the outside, with a few purple lines inside, and instead of the little pillar the central ridge bulges out, which is yellow and slimy. All five come together at the bottom, and fashion a pointed little bag like larkspurs,[16] so that the stem is penetrated[17] at the side. It has little smell.

The fruit is a finger joint long, the thickness of a quill, triangular, and each side has three ridges, on the inside filled with yellow marrow, like the foregoing. The root also produces several small purses, striped as before, which in time produce their own stems. It thrives on old, rotten trees, that grow on open hillsides,[18] and which have fallen down, near *Caju puti*[19] forests.

It does not sit straight on the branches, but as if glued to it from the side, and its stems, which are five or six inches long, come at an angle from the tree, and partly hang down; the root has another strange growth added onto it,[20] that covers some of

Tab. XLIV.

Fig. 1.

Fig. 2.

the selfsame's tufts of hair,[21] in the shape of a horned Worm, or Caterpillar, plant-like, brittle, savorless, like Polypodium.[22] The stems that come out first are sometimes folded double, with the tip curved down.

Name. In Latin *Angraecum album minus*; in Malay, *Angrec puti kitsjil*[23] or *Angrec cassian*,[24] which means *Poor Angrek,* from its simple[25] shape, a name also given to the large variety. One could call it *Beursjes angrec* [Angrec Purses] in Dutch, after the shape of the flower.

Place. It also grows on wild trees, like the large one, but is not seen as often, it is also found on old, rotten, and fallen trees, but neither can be easily transplanted, because the roots are too hard, and spread out too far.

This small kind has yet another variation,[26] making for a mixed form with *Daun subat*.[27] For it has a thin, prone stem that grows downwards, that sends some threads from its joints, wherewith it fastens itself, and upwards several other stems without bellies, partially bare, thereafter four, five or six thick stiff leaflets, smaller than the ones described above; the stem has yet another foot in length, as thick as an oaten straw, at the top putting forth two flowers, like the foregoing, having a somewhat pleasant smell.

The Forty Third Plate.

Shows the *large white Angrec.*

The Forty Fourth Plate.

The first Figure shows the *small white Angrek,* which is the Pennangu Maravara in the *H. Malab. 12. vol. Tab. 3.*[28]

The second Figure indicates the *red Angrek,* which is described in the next Chapter.

Chapter Three

THE RED ANGREK.

The fourth kind of Angrec[1] is the red one, which has only one species, even more ropy[2] than the foregoing, for it is a long rope that runs with long branches through tangled thickets,[3] but one will not find its root anchored in the ground, but here and there on an old rotten tree; the branches are the thickness of one's little finger, round, hard, and stiff, but snap readily when broken off; they bear the leaves, and not in separate tufts like the first kind, but on this flower-bearing stem [itself] alternately above each other, four or five inches long, two wide, very thick and stiff, with a slight bulge near the stem, a blunt tip, divided into two, otherwise without ridges, except that, from below, one can see the central sinew protrude a little.

The stem that bears the flowers, has the length of two and a half spans,[4] round, stiff, divided into various side branches that bear the flowerlets; these are the size of common Hyacinths, crowded together, at right angles from the stem, fashioned from five small leaflets, of which the two broadest ones are curved down, and the three narrower ones are curved upwards, with a bright yellow background, flecked with red lines and dots, so that the entire cluster seems to be fiery red, with a small purse or cup of the same color in the center. Their disposition is not the same, for the widest leaves are now on top and then below.

The flower-bearing stem has red lines as well; the leaves taste somewhat sour and slightly salty.

The fruits are easily a finger joint long, half a finger thick, both back and front are pointed, with a dirty yellow color, somewhat triangular, but with six protruding ridges, striped lengthwise, and inside one will see the same yellow fibrous marrow as in the other Angreks, and the rest of the flower is on top, being a six-leaved starlet.

Name. In Latin *Angraecum rubrum;*[5] in Malay *Angrec mera;* the Ambonese have no specific name for it.

Place. It grows mostly on the beach, with its many tendrils creeping through the shrubbery, although it will always have a rotten piece of wood or old root as its place of origin. One will also find it running up trees in valleys, and along rivers, where its fiery red amidst the green offers a beautiful spectacle.

Use. It has no general use, except that one can place the young leaves in Vinegar and Salt, either by themselves or mixed with some Atsjaar,[6] when they will taste like Cappars,[7] but you cannot suck on them much, because they are too fibrous, and you will get little more than the taste of Cappers. One should choose the thickest and fattest leaves for this purpose, ones that grow on the beach and in more open thickets, for these will have a pleasant saltiness, and are to be preferred to the ones from the forest.

This *Angraecum rubrum*[8] has a variation or commingled shape with the subsequent *Octavum sive furvum*.[9] The leaves are somewhat larger, five or six inches long, two wide, with a double tip, the flowers are red, yellow, or orange, similar to the dried Mace of Nutmegs, without points, also with five leaflets, of which the two broadest ones hang down, and the other three stand upright, and the flower cluster is divided into several small side branches. One does not see this species on trees, like the other Angreks, but it grows on the beach in the thickets, with long woody twigs like ropes, similar to the foregoing, which have a spongy and watery marrow inside.

But I cannot say, however, that these two kinds spring from the ground, for they run so far through the thickest shrubs, that one cannot reach the root, and the few I encountered, had established themselves on old rotten stumps and decayed twigs.

Chapter Four

THE FIFTH ANGREK.

This fifth kind[1] is a small subspecies of the first or large one, but due to its difference I gave it a separate chapter. First of all, it has a large bunch of leaves, which grow in a particular manner, all together, and embracing one another, fourteen or fifteen inches long, two wide; the front tip is markedly split in two, and one of these corners is longer than the other. Next to this gathering, a flower-bearing stem comes from the root itself, round, stiff, four feet long, with rather limp flowers, alternately one above the other, on curved stems.

The flowers resemble those of the first kind, but smaller, opened further, fashioned from five leaflets, purple or a light purple on the outside, yellow on the inside, with blood-red drops, or thick characters, whereof some are round, like drops, others oblong, and other ones have a little yellow spot in the center. There is a tiny helmet in the center, with two angles on either side, like tiny horns, white with purple lines, and in front of this is another curved little horn, with a groove inside, the color of purple on top, yellow below. The edges of the thick leaflets are usually curled over, and the knop of the curled flower is purple as well. The flower has no scent on Ambon, but it does on Bali, if one opens the central helmet. The characters of this flower are oblong at the base, like stripes, wide towards the front, angular, and some enclose a small yellow circle.

Its fruits are oblong pods, hexagonal, three or four fingers long, one finger thick, with yellow meal inside, like the foregoing.

Name. In Latin *Angraecum quintum, sive Angraecum scriptum minus;*[2] in Malay and Balinese *Angrek kringsing kitsjil.*

Place. It grows on the beach on *Mangium caseolare,*[3] or *Waccat,*[4] with its stems sometimes hanging down so low that they touch the water, for these trees stand in the sea when the tide is coming in, and are dry at ebb tide, whence I guess the Malay call this flower *Renda*[5] *casian,*[6] that is to say humble, and poor, because they droop so meekly. One can keep cut ones for a long time inside. The Balinese often plant this one and the first kind on *Sajor puti*[7] trees, whereon they wax luxuriously, and which they accomplish as follows. They cut the entire stock from the mother trunk, with part of the selfsame bark, then they tie it with Gomuto ropes[8] on the thick branches of the aforementioned trees, and smear them with mud on the outside, and they will grow firmly onto it.

Chapter Five

THE YELLOW ANGREK.

T he sixth, seventh, eighth, ninth, and tenth kinds of An-grek are those, that have yellow flowers, with few or no characters, differing from the foregoing in that the leaves are not in separate tufts, but grow onto or next to the flower-bearing stem, but they also divide into branches, and there are a large number of them, of which we will describe two in this chapter.

I. *Angraecum sextum Moschatum sive odoratum,*[1] also attaches itself to the bark of trees, with many, thick, and white fibers, which also make for a clump wherefrom one or two stems shoot up, three feet high, with the lower third clothed in leaves, growing alternately above one another, almost in two rows, the one in the lap of the other, thick and stiff, almost like those of the Houseleek,[2] four inches long, two fingers wide, without sinews or veins, except that one can see a groove on the inner side.

The tip is split in two, and the front half is always a little longer; beyond this the stem becomes bellied and striped, a fin-ger thick, four inches long; the remainder is as thick as a quill, not quite round, with uneven joints, divided on top into three or four side branches.

But the flowers have their own particular shape; first of all, they have two long, narrow leaflets, like the spatules[3] of Surgeons, bent backwards at the top, and slightly curled, the length of one's little finger; next to them are three broader leaflets spread out in a triangle, at first pale or a greenish yellow, like the Cananga flower,[4] thereafter a true yellow, and slightly striped from below, without characters, though sometimes with purple lines on one side, and in the center one will see another leaflet, at the sides divided into four angles or joints, and folded together like a chalice, whitish and beautifully adorned with purple lines, and on the selfsame's top stands the little thick center pillar with a yellow little head. It has a fairly sweet scent at dawn, when the flower first opens up, almost like Narcissi, or the Tanjong flowers[5] in this country, faint, but stronger than other kinds of Angreks.

It has an even more lovely scent on Bali,[6] wherefore they fabulate that Dewa,[7] which is their God, called Dewata, Lewata, Rewata, and Rewa by other Indian Heathens, visits the flower at night and bestrews it with some Muscus[8] or Civet, which gave it its name. The flower-bearing stem does not shoot up straight from the gathering of the leaves, but often sideways from among them, as if it had been stuck between them.

The fruit is, as before, fashioned from the foot of the flower, shorter than the former kind, one and a half inch long, one inch thick, triangular, though each side has a lower edge, green as grass, with a downy yellow meal inside, keeping the dried flower on top for a long time.[9]

Name. In Latin *Angraecum sextum Moschatum, sive odoratum;* in

Malay and Balinese *Angrec casturi;*[10] because it smells like Muscus. Most of them on Ternate share the same name with the foregoing *Saja boki,* or *Saja ngawa ngawan.*[11] This kind has the most in common with *Helleborine recentiorum,*[12] because it bears its leaves on the stem, and because they are small.

Place. It sits on trees like the *Waccat, Mangium caseolare,*[13] and the Lemon trees that grow in Ambonese forest gardens.

II. *Angraecum septimum*[14] has well-nigh the same leaves, or slightly larger, five or six inches long, three wide, arranged alternately closely on top of each other, with three dark sinews, striped lengthwise, whereof the central one is a groove. Normally a flower-bearing stem shoots forth from the side of this gathering; it is an ell,[15] or two feet long, a little bellied below, on top scarcely the thickness of a quill, woody, round, sprinkled with brown lines, whereon grow the flowers, somewhat thin, many on top of each other, on longish stems.

The flowers resemble a flying horsefly,[16] fashioned from five leaflets, of which the top one is slightly curled forward, resembling [the horsefly's] back; the other two would be the wings; two others on the side are shorter, and cover a central leaflet, which has two flaps at the side, which encircle the little central pillar; the outer leaves are somewhat striped like the Kananga flower,[17] yellow on the outside, a bright yellow inside, like the Tsjampacca flower;[18] the little helmet has a rim like a tongue, bent outwards, and striped with purple lines. The lower part of the flower resembles a horn, like a Larkspur, representing the horsefly's head, almost odorless.

The fruit is thinner, and more oblong than the foregoing,

Tab. XLV.

scarcely the thickness of a finger, striped with six edges, filled inside with the usual yellow meal.

The flower remains vigorous for a long time, until the foot begins to thicken; then the outer leaflets close up, and hide the helmet, which has already turned red.[19] It blooms in the rainy season. The leaves have a sour taste, mixed with a saltiness, and it blunts the teeth.

Name. In Latin *Angraecum septimum;*[20] in Malay *Angrec tsjam-pacca.*[21]

Place. This too grows on beaches on the aforementioned Mangi-Mangi trees,[22] as well as on others that stand in salt water or salt creeks.

The Forty Fifth Plate.

Shows the *seventh,* or the yellow *Angrek,* which was described as the second kind in this Chapter.

The roots of *Angraecum octavum sive Furvum*[1] are more spread out than the former, and hang loosely from the trees; the leaves grow in the same manner in two rows, but they are eight and nine inches long, scarcely one wide, also split in two at the tips, without sinews, except for the central groove, with the same taste as the foregoing. The flower-bearing stem shoots up as well as to the side, and the latter sends some roots or fibers down, which also attach themselves to the bark of the tree.

The central or main stem is also bellied, in such a way that it is always thinner between its place of origin and the belly, which is the case with all the Angreks that have bellied stems.

The flowers appear on an expansive cluster, on rather long-ish dirty-white stems, fashioned from five leaflets, opened wide, curved like half moons; some are also curled, the size of *Angraecum tertium*[2] or *Rubrum*,[3] yellowish on the outside, dark inside, russet or a smoky color, yellow at the edges, with a sweet though faint odor, that has a hint of dog in it, like the Satyria. In the center is a leaflet like a tooth, pale yellow, with two white little flaps below, ending at the bottom in a short purse; in front of these is a little pillar or anvil, also yellow, and between them two white leaflets. One can keep cut stems and flowers for a long time.

The fruits of *Angraecum furvum* are hexagonal pods, a hand wide, and long, easily a finger thick, divided into six ridges, inside with the same kind of yellow and hairy marrow, that has yellow, fine sand hanging from it. It creeps through everything, and it has long, curved roots behind the leaves, like strings, round, two feet long, the thickness of a quill, tough and breakable, with two or three divisions in front.

Name. In Latin *Angraecum octavum* or *Furvum;* in Malay *Angreck kitsjil glap.*[4]

Place. It grows on the aforementioned Wakkat trees, on both living and dead trunks, and on half-rotted branches. It does not transplant easily due to its expansive roots, as was the case with *Angraecum album.*[5]

Angraecum nonum[6] has the smallest leaves, similar to our common *Sempervivum,*[7] about a finger long, scarcely two wide, without sinews, except for a dark groove, not much split at the tips, thick, and stiff, with an unpleasant sour taste. The leaf-bearing stem sometimes has an oblong belly under the leaves, not angular or striped lengthwise, but transversely divided into dark joints. The flower-bearing stems arise on top as well as to the sides, and the flowers resemble the sixth kind[8] the most, though usually smaller, so that it looks like a smaller version of it. For the five outer leaflets are a pale yellow with light purple lines. The little helmet is whitish with purple lines, and ends below in a little horn just like the Larkspurs; before noon it spreads a lovely scent, though faint, which is like the flower of the *Orchis,* or *Bonga tanjong*[9] in this country.

The plant's main stems are only three feet tall, and the other stems grow like those of *Daun subat,*[10] slightly brown by the joints; it grows on wild trees around Capaha,[11] flowering in November and December, and was specifically called *Angrek lemon kitsjil*[12] because, like the large one, it loves to grow on Lemon trees.

Angraecum decimum or *Angustifolium*[13] is the tiniest one, mostly growing on Kanari trees,[14] with thick, narrow leaves, like the pods of *Catjang tsjina,*[15] six or seven inches long, not round, but flat, the width of a quill, and disposed around the straight stem. The flowers are very small, two or three together from the lap of the leaves, a pale yellow, fashioned from five leaflets, of which the upper two, which are also the narrowest ones, hang down and over, with a little purple helmet inside.

The fruit is the thickness of a quill, triangular, but striped in between, one and a half fingers long, with the remaining flower on top; it does not grow taller than a foot; growing under Ferns on Mangi Mangi, or wild trees, the root is thinner[16] and long.

Bontius Lib.6 Cap. 36.[17] describes a similar plant, which he calls *Sedum arborescens,* that has a wondrously knobby root, which he compares with the shaft of a Turkish spear, with thick leaves like the Houseleek, and small white flowers like Anagallis, very fragrant like Lemon peels, and the leaves taste as sour as those of Sorel. He ascribes it many excellent virtues, which were tried by the Javanese, for they made a Conserva[18] from the leaves, said to be a boon for all brain ailments, and nerves, such as

Tab. XLVI.

Fig. 2.

Fig. 1.

Spasmum and Cholerum; the flowers fortify the heart, and the leaves cure bloody flux, since they are cold, kind of sour, and of an astringent nature. The leaves are also supposed to be very effective against poisoned wounds from krisses and pikes.

The fruit is the length of one's middle finger, slimy inside, and insipid, and if the fruit is cut across one will see a Fort with four Bulwarks.

The Forty Sixth Plate.

The first Figure shows the dark *Angrek* or the eighth one. The second Figure depicts the *ninth kind* of *Angrek*.

Chapter Seven

THE DOG ANGREK.

The eleventh kind also has many long roots that are all tangled up, and which wind around a tree without forming a massive clump. But from the center arise two or three stems, that are striped below and leaved for a length of eighteen to twenty inches. These leaves grow in two rows, alternately over against one another, at a straight angle from the stem, stiff and ribbed, four to five inches long, one and a half wide.

The remainder of the stem is bare, somewhat bellied below, otherwise round, and two or three feet long, bearing few flowers at the tip, two or three together. These are, along with the white ones, the largest among all the Angreks, fashioned from five leaves, all purple, without characters, of which the four outer leaves are spread out. The sixth stands over the little chalice like a thimble, truly purple, and woolly on the inside, like an Iris, hiding a tiny pillar in the center, without a horn below. The flower has a strong smell, cloying,[1] grievous to the head, and markedly doggish, like the flowers of certain Satyria.

The taste is salty, tart, but not unpleasant, and it does not produce purses from its root, nor bellied stems, like other An-

Tab. XLVII.

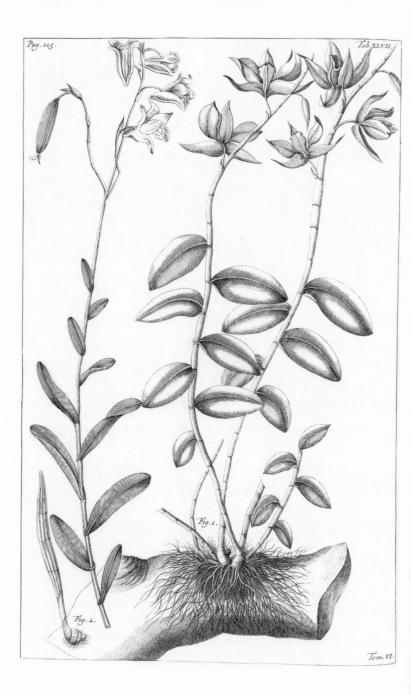

Fig. 1.

Fig. 2.

greks; one sees the fruits in October and November, and they are angular like the other Angreks.

Name. In Latin *Angraecum caninum, sive Undecimum;*[2] in Malay *Angreck andjing*[3] because of its doggish smell.

Place. It grows on trees that have a short, thick trunk, and are mossy, especially on Kinar trees,[4] both on beaches and in the valleys; otherwise no use is known.

The Forty Seventh Plate.

Shows the *Dog Angrek* with the first Figure.

The second Figure points out the *pursed Angrek* described in Chapter 57 of the *Auctuarium.*[5]

THE FIFTY SEVENTH CHAPTER
OF THE AUCTUARIUM
GIVES THE FOLLOWING NEW KINDS OF
ANGREKS.

One should not think that Ambon's luxuriant wilder-
nesses produce no other kinds of Angreks, besides the
ones, which we proposed at the beginning of book eleven, when
I gave up hope to find out about all of them; since then I have
found some new kinds, which I deemed worthy to be described,
because of their rare appearance, and I will present some of
them here one after another.[1]

I. *Angraecum nervosum,*[2] which grows on Kinar[3] and Ironwood[4]
trees, appears with many square purses, three to four inches
long, two fingers thick, heaped together in groups, of a pale
green color, and somewhat hard, like all the others. Each purse
produces a large leaf, twelve to fifteen inches long, four or five
wide, striped lengthwise with five sinews, which make for sharp
ridges below, and which looks like those of *Helleborus albus;*[5] over
against each leaf is a small pointed leaflet, and from its center
comes a stem, about a foot long, round, the thickness of oaten
pipe, whereon grow three or four flowerlets, which at first are
long pointed knops.

The flower resembles those of other Angreks of average
size, consisting of five leaflets, of which the three outer and

largest ones have a whitish-yellow color, whereof one stands up straight, and two hang down, then there are two narrow ones like small thongs, which bend backwards; inside one will find the usual little house, fashioned from two leaflets, white on the outside, veering towards yellow, with brown speckles inside.

This flower resembles a flying Horsefly, if one takes the angular little stem to be the head, the lowest broad leaflet the tail, and the two narrow leaflets the wings.[6]

The fruits are still not known, unless they are produced by the flower's angular foot; the taste of the leaves is bitter and unpleasant. It is, therefore, a singular Angrek because it has striped leaves, and the flower stem comes from the purse itself.

The Forty Eighth Plate.[7]

Shows the *sinewy Angrek*, which might possibly be the Erythro-bulb, with folded leaves of the white Helleborus, Red bulb, as we call it in *Plukn. Mantiss.*[8] p. 70 and the Chichultic Tepetlauhxochite of *Hernand.* in *Recch.*[9] p. 368.

II. *Angraecum pungens*,[10] or stinging Angrek, found on a Caju matta buta[11] tree, does not acquire a purse, but creeps with a thick tendril along the branches, and hangs down mostly, shooting up a stem here and there, that bears the leaves, and between them other ones appear.

The leaves grow singly, twelve to fourteen inches long, scarcely the width of one's little finger, with a point in front, about a finger joint long, which seems as if it had been placed there, otherwise thick, stiff, and without noticeable sinews,

Tab. XLVIII.

which protrude somewhat at the bottom, and make the leaf slightly hollow at the top, like a flat groove, of a dark green color, and the older ones turn russet; the stinging tips drop off the old leaves, between the same appear other thin, stiff and woody little stems out of the main stem, four or five inches long, some of them dividing into two little stems to the side; the front half is covered with flowers, shaped like the normal Angreks, but with short leaves, and a yellowish white.

The fruit comes forth from its stem, barely an inch long, striped, triangular, in the shape of a budding Clove,[12] bearing flowers on top for a long time, filled inside with a coarse, whitish meal.

III. *Angraecum saxatile*[13] or Rock Angrek, is almost the same ropy plant, that crawls over rocks; the leaves grow together in tufts, eight to ten inches long, one wide, grooved on top, below with a sharp ridge, split in two at the front, with two tips, of which one is not only noticeably longer than the other, but also stings like a soft thorn.

Long, round, and somewhat crooked stems emerge between the back leaves, like Girdles, tough, and unbreakable, white on the outside, and dividing at the end into two or three branches, which in turn root themselves in the bark of the trees.

The Forty Ninth Plate.

The first Figure shows the *Rock Angrek,* which is the Tsjerou mau maravara of the *H. Malab. part. 12. Tab. 5*[14] to which *Plukn.* in *Almag. p. 87.*[15] added the Monomotapense Caryophyllus with

Tab. XLIX.

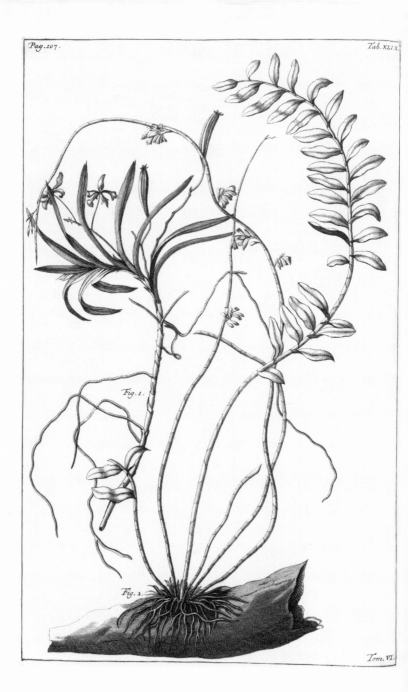

Fig. 1.

Fig. 2.

the sinewy leaves of the Bupleurum, hollow inside, with a blue flower, and with small stems winged lengthwise,[16] in *Phyt. Tab. 275. fig. 1.*[17]

A Parasytic plant belongs to this as well, quite similar to the Orchis, with a thickly formed leaf in *Herm. Parud. Bat. p. 187.*[18] Though the flower differs somewhat: which is the American Viscum that grows on trees, with a beautiful white flower, and leaves in the shape of Nerium Pods in *Plukn. Phyt. Tab. 117. fig. 6.*

The second Figure shows the *purple Angrek*, described in *Chapter Eight,* to wit, the first kind.

IV. *Angraecum angustis crumenis,*[19] acquires many, roundish purses divided into two or three dark joints, five or six inches long, easily one wide, draped with many dry little fleeces on the outside; most are bare and without leaves, others bear three or four long, narrow leaves on top, twelve to fifteen inches long, two fingers wide, coming to a single point, except for the central sinew, bulging slightly at the bottom, and with some stripes like very fine sinews down the length of them.

Next to this tuft of leaves they have two leaf-bearing stems, also fifteen inches long, which bear the flowerlets on the front half, [which are] as yet unknown. Followed by the fruits, scarcely an inch long, an oaten pipe thick, the root is a clump of thin, long, and very tough fibers.

V. *Angraecum sediforme,*[20] really called such because the leaves look like those of the Sedum or Houseleek;[21] some are one, others are three inches long, two fingers wide, some without ridges, with a stiff point, thick, smooth, and sappy, though without milk, otherwise one would think it was a *Nummularia lactea.*[22] The flower has not been seen yet. It grows with thin and entangled chords under and through the roots of other Angreks.

VI. *Angraecum uniflorum*[23] has leaves that, in terms of shape and size, resemble a tongue, to wit, round in front, and somewhat split in two, thick, stiff, and without ridges, except for a flat groove on the upper side. Every leaf rests on a short little purse, made from four or five sharp ridges, some also smooth with two sides.

The flower stem appears next to the purse, round, a span high, each one bearing just one flower, somewhat similar to *Angrec angin,*[24] fashioned from three leaves, of which the largest and frontal one has the shape of a tongue, wide in back, narrow in front, with a sharp ridge in the center, curved backwards over the entire flower; to the side are two other leaves, also broad in back, and thick, narrow in front, curved toward each other like sickles.

There is a tiny little head in the center. Its color is brown, with many white-yellow stipples or eyelets on it, some round, some square, otherwise odorless.

It grows with a simple root on the branches of wild trees, and sometimes forms a flat corner, as if fashioned from Moss, wherefrom here and there the little purses and some leaves emerge.

VII. *Angrec gajang*[25] was found on a Gajang tree,[26] together with many small bushes, has the shape of a *Javanese Lily,* or *Casi selan,*[27] at the bottom with an oblong globule, like an Onion. This one produces two leaves, scarcely twelve inches long, and one wide, with a stiff central sinew on the underside, and with-out a split tip, as other Angreks have, though it does come to a point.

A single, long stem emerges from between these two leaves, of which the upper and greatest half, easily a foot long, is covered with flowerlets, which look just like the Angreks, fash-ioned from five dirty-white, narrow leaflets, of which three hang down, and two spread out, with a little helmet on the upper side. It also has a pointed leaflet where its stem begins, and this covers the stem. They grow so closely together, that the entire stem looks like a long cattail,[28] and after they fall off a few fruits come to perfection, which are the tiniest of all the Angreks, to wit, slightly larger than a wheat kernel, hex-agonal, bursting open when they ripen, except that the front one remains hanging together. What is inside is first yellowish, and sappy, and this changes in the ripe ones into a sandy yellow meal.

It blooms in the rainy season, and one will find it on Gajang trees, that grow in the wild in the valley of Ayer Cotta Lamma.[29] One will find this kind also on other trees, on the East Coast of Celebes as well, where they use the leaves for swollen and hardened bellies, withered[30] over a fire, so they become soft, and then rubbed on the stomach, and the marrow of the narrow globules are chewed in the mouth, and the sap swallowed.

VIII. *Angrec jambu*[31] has narrow, stiff leaves, five inches long, two fingers wide, ending up front in a stiff point; its taste is unpleasant at first, but then becomes sweet like the sap of Lico-rice.

The flowerlets grow on the tendril two by two, over against one another, on short little feet, fashioned from five thick Lemon-yellow leaflets, all curved inwards like birds' claws, and in the center one will see a purplish-blue little tongue. The fruits are still not known, and it grows with long dangling tendrils on wild Jambu trees.[32]

IX. *Angraecum taeniosum,*[33] or thonged[34] Angrec, has a single, woody stem, with its leaves disposed on it singly and without order, resembling thick little thongs, with a groove lengthwise on either side, as if they had been fashioned from two parts, four to five inches long, and easily the thickness of an oaten pipe. From the sides of the front leaves comes a short flower cluster, but the flowers are still not known.

These are followed by three to six fruits, being oblong, ridged pods, a thumb joint long, like the other Angreks, divided on the outside into three larger and three smaller, sharp ridges, with a tiny crown on top, being the remainder of the flower, filled inside with a sandy lint. The root is long, thin, woody, and creeps forward at an angle; it does not produce a purse.

X. *Angraecum lanuginosum,*[35] differs slightly from the normal Angrek shape, for it acquires a single stem, three to four feet long, without a belly or purse, of which the back half is bare, and divided into dark joints. The front half is thickly leafed, round, and woolly.

The leaves have the shape of the small Angreks, growing very irregularly around the stem, three or four inches long, two fingers wide, thick, stiff, without a noticeable sinew, ending in a short, stiff point, that is slightly crooked.

The upper side is a little coarse, like worn plush, and of the three or four top ones, the youngest ones are woolly on either side.

The flower stem emerges from the lap of the foremost leaves, easily a finger long, whereon grow the flowerlets on short little feet, also woolly, the size of a Bean.

They have on the bottom a round leaflet like a little boat, wherein lies a round flowerlet that opens up into three yellowish thick leaflets, with a tiny purple tongue sticking out between them, together resembling a Lion's mouth with a protruding tongue.[36]

It has a sparse root, fashioned from a few fibers, and grows beneath other Angreks on wild trees, at Toleeuw,[37] a Village in Eastern Ambon.

Chapter Eight

THE PURPLE ANGREK.

The twelfth kind was so rarely seen with leaves, that many thought it was leafless. I have found this difference, to wit, the one that grows on trees and on rocks on the beach, is usually seen without leaves, but the one that grows on trees inland, does have leaves, so that one could make them into two kinds, which is not necessary, however, since there is too little difference between them.

I. First of all, the beach kind[1] has an angular or striped stem, divided into many uneven joints, that are always thicker in the center than at the ends, just as the entire stem below, near the root, is at its thinnest and roundest, bearing leaves like the foregoing little Angreks, growing alternately above one another, five inches long, easily one wide, and split in front like the others.

This stem becomes about a foot tall, and has only leaves which fall off, when they have grown old, leaving the bare stem behind, and this causes people to think that it is leafless, for to the side of the aforementioned stem comes yet another particular one from the root, two to three feet high, thinner down below, near the root, thereafter divided into similar bellied joints. The flowerlets grow where these joints come together, which are always lower than the belly, hanging together in clusters, like vertebrae, or Jambu flowers,[2] around the joints or bare on one side.

These flowerlets have a particular shape, different from the foregoing, for they have five leaflets, that are not open, but closed together as if forming a little pipe, open on the underside, with a tiny little bag or horn nearby, as with the Orchides, an inch long or less, scarcely an oaten pipe thick. The upper edges are divided into tips, and inside the hindmost two leaflets cover a little helmet, the color of purple or a rose-red, like the color Cassomba,[3] with no scent whatsoever. These clusters hang from the center of the stem, and near the tips it is almost bare; the fruits are still not known, the root is paltry, fashioned from short fibers.

This kind is found on the beach, on both short and thick trees, as well as on steep rocks, that have pieces of rotten wood or twigs scattered about on them.

Name. It is specifically called *Angrecum Purpureum* or *nudum*,[4] in Malay *Angrek Jambu*,[5] or *Angrek Cassumba;*[6] *Rangrec* in Javanese, as they call all other Angreks.

II. The land kind[7] does not differ from the foregoing except that it shows more leaves, because from a root that is thin, mossy and fibrous, come eight to ten stems, eight to nine feet long, of which the thicker ones bear the leaves, and the thinner ones the flowers, divided into many joints, that do not have any peculiar bumps, like the foregoing, but are deeply grooved and striped.

The leaves on the stems begin at least four feet from the

root, and then only singly and alternately, many on top of one another, thinner than other Angreks, five to six inches long, two fingers wide, coming to a point, with a central sinew protruding below, with an insipid and viscous taste. The part of the stem that bears the leaves, is thicker than below.

The flower-bearing stem has its flowers around the center; these are like round globules and hang together in groups, now on one then on the other side of the stem; every flowerlet is about a fingernail long, like a tiny chalice, scarcely as thick as a quill, with a pointed little sack at the bottom that is striped, or divisible into narrow leaflets, which open up on top with five tips, and show inside a whitish, stiff little chalice, while they themselves are a purple-red, scentless; one will see them in October and November.

Name. In Latin *Angraecum purpureum silvestre;*[8] in Malay *Angrec cassomba,* or *Jambu; Rangrec* in Javanese, like the foregoing.

Place. It grows on wild trees, such as Waringin[9] trees, Samaria[10] or Clove[11] trees.

Use. Crush the stems, heat them, and smear it on, which will cure *Matta ican,*[12] or whitlow of the hands and fingers, to wit, when it will not burst, in order to divide and destroy the swelling, or otherwise to break it up when it has grown large.

On tall forest trees these stems grow to be seven or eight feet long, from the bottom up mostly bare, flowers in the center, and at the upper end again with some leaves; they are filled with a tough slime, which will flow copiously when cut or broken, yet they cannot be ripped off because they are very tough. They are round near the root, thereafter deeply edged or striped, and

Tab. I.

A

Fig. 2.

Fig. 3.

Fig. 1.

in front, between the leaves, roundishly flat, with two ridges on the sides.

Some other kinds of Angreks, which I came to know about at a later time, were discussed in the foregoing chapter, *Ch. 57* of the *Auctuar.*

The Fiftieth Plate.

The first Figure shows the *purple Angrek,* to wit, its *second kind,* described in this *eighth Chapter.*

The second Figure shows the *Beseeching Plant,*[13] to wit, its *first kind,* which comes close to resembling the Thalia Maravara in the *H. Malab. part.12. Tab. 4.*[14]

The third Figure depicts the other *wild* or *peasant Angrek,* described in the *eleventh Chapter,* with its *fruit* shown by A.

Chapter Nine

THE BESEECHING PLANT.

This plant also wants to be part of the Angrek family, and it can serve that Aristocracy as a Parasite[1] or Flatterer, who usually follows the court, and it has five kinds, a small or ordinary one, and four large ones.

I. *Herba supplex minor,*[2] is a little plant, no more than half a foot tall, sprouting from the root with almost no stems, for they begin at the bottom soon after the root, on a very short little stem, two rows of leaves over against one another, one embracing the other alternately, completely flat, as if they had been pressed.

Each leaflet is a thumb joint long, barely half a finger wide, stiff and rather thick, coming at an angle from its congregation, at the lower sides straight or only slightly curved, but the upper side is bellied, which makes the leaf wider in the center than at the back, in the shape of a Saber or a crescent Moon. They appear to be double at the hind end, straight as if a leaf was folded lengthwise, but they are whole[3] on the front edges, a bright sea-green, smooth on the outside, fibrous inside, and with a salty taste, that has some tartness in it, remaining alive for a long time[4] after it has been broken off and hung in the house.

Eight or ten of these leaflets grow in a row, and the central ones are the largest. But such congregations grow only four, six or seven [of them] together, on their thin little stems, from a trifling root, fashioned from Mossy fibers, with which it clings to the bark of a tree so firmly, that one can usually pull the leaflets off without [removing] the roots. Most of the time one usually sees only these leaves on it, but when it has become truly old, it produces its flowers and seeds.

The flowerlets are small, barely the size of Lilies of the Valley,[5] peeping out singly between the leaflets, for these are short, narrow, little chalices, a deep brown,[6] with sharp upper edges, standing in a small, green-bearded chalice, whereafter follow grain kernels, like rice grains, keeping the dry flowers on top for a long time, filled inside with a pale yellow and hairy meal, like the other Angreks.

It grows on trees such as the *Mangium caseolare,* or *Waccat,* on the beach, also on *Waringin* trees, and on other beach trees that have a somewhat slanted trunk.

Name. In Latin *Herba supplex minor,* in Malay *Daun subat;*[7] one has to distinguish it from another *Daun subat,* which we described earlier as a kind of grass in the beginning of book ten,[8] wherefore the Ternatans gave it another name.

II. *Herba supplex major prima,*[9] also has several stems from one root, that are partly bare at the bottom, thereafter decked with leaves to a height of two feet, of the same shape as the foregoing, but larger, then the stem grows for another foot or foot and a half, draped at the top with tiny flowers, which are yellow, and look like a small helmet, and that drop readily, leaving the bare stem behind; only a few become fruits, which are triangular berries, filled with the usual yellow meal.

The people in *Luhu* call it specifically *Sibane*, others *Daun subat parampuan*,[10] that is to say *Herba supplex femina*, for they consider the foregoing one the *male*.

Use. Both kinds got their names, because the leaflets are joined together like the fingers of two hands, as if to pray, to wit, when one turns the leafy bunches upside down; a similar reason was mentioned for the aforementioned *Daun subat* grass.

The Malay and the people from Hitu use them because of this shape, just as the Ternatans do with the aforementioned grass, to wit, for lovers to send to each other, when they want to beseech one another, or beg for forgiveness, and they use this even more specifically, in that the men should send the leaf of the first kind, which has the stiffest leaflets, showing thereby more desire.[11]

But the second, and subsequent kinds, are sent by the women, thereby admitting, that their beseeching and begging is less sincere and more of a pretense than with the men.

The Reader is requested not to laugh too much at such trifles, since here, in the Indies, it is often very useful to understand this Hieroglyphic Grammar,[12] in order not to be cheated.

The Alfurs on Ceram stick these leaved stems with the flowers in their armbands,[13] which they wear on their arms when they go plundering or hunting for heads, because they believe it will make them brave, or have good luck, I presume because they think that these plants are lucky due to their durable fresh green.

III. *Herba supplex major secunda*,[14] was also held to be the female, and has more in common with that Gramen supplex,[15] since it has much thinner and narrower leaves than the two foregoing, wherefore it is much more like a grass. They are also fitted into each other;[16] each leaflet is five inches long, and less, and has a little knee in the center, but they are mostly withered, and eaten through towards the front; next to these leafy tufts grow very thin, stiff little stems, which, while creeping along, form little knees, root themselves, and produce new bunches of leaves, emerging not straight from the little stems, but on the sides, always forming smaller bunches all the way to the end. It grows on the beach on old trees that are bent forward a little, also on rocks that have some soil on them, and get good sunlight.

IV. *Herba supplex major tertia*,[17] acquires angular and slightly bulging stems below, near the root, divided into sharp ridges, like the Angrek. The leaves are like those of the second kind of Herba supplex, and grow in bunches together, pressed flat, but in such a way, that they divide on top into two or three other bunches, and the upper stem shoots up a ways with some leaves, up to the top stem, that bears sparse flowers, like the second kind; after the flowers the knobby stems are bare, with a fruit dangling from a thin stem here and there, triangular, but the spaces between them are divided into ridges, a fingernail long, with a yellow meal inside.

V. *Herba supplex major quarta*,[18] has leaves and stems like the

Tab. LI.

Fig. 2.

Fig. 1.

second one, though usually larger; the stems are an ell high, and more, with a few leaves on them; it also bears on top only two or three flowers, curved like crescent moons, each one open on its own little thin stem, like a little boat or shoe.[19] The lowest leaflet grows upwards, divided into five points, which look like shoeheels; at the top is yet another leaflet bent backwards like the nose of a shoe, entirely white, with some yellow inside on the upper leaflet, scentless.

Herba supplex quinta[20] is better described as hanging like a rope from the trees, grows with fourteen or sixteen stems out of one root, thin at its point of origin, flat, and very tough; three of them grow up to the length of a fathom, and more, and produce short side branches at the top, which are disposed transversely. The leaves are a finger long, scarcely one wide, stiff, with a long tip, fashioned like a Lance; the flower is the size of a small Angrek, the same shape as above: The fruit is still unknown. There is a depiction of it.[21]

The Fifty First Plate.

Shows the *Beseeching Plant* in the first Figure, to wit, the *female,* or the *second kind.*[22]

The second Figure shows the *fifth kind* of the *Beseeching Plant,* hanging down from the wood that it grows on, with the actual shape and size of its flower.

Chapter Ten

THE FIRST GROUND ANGREK.

Now follows the Peasant kin of the Angreks, which, unlike the previous twelve,[1] do not grow in trees, but on the ground, and which are once again divided into various kinds, whereof some come close to resembling the Helleborus plant, and others the Orchis or Standelwort.[2] The first class has four kinds, and we devote a chapter to each one. The first one is *Angrecum terrestre primum*, the second *Angrecum terrestre alterum*, the third *Involucrum*, and the fourth *Helleborus Amboinicus*.

I. *Angraecum terrestre primum*,[3] or *Daun corra corra*,[4] sprouts from the ground, and it attaches itself by means of many thick fibers, that mostly creep bare along the ground, like worms, and it has countless other, smaller ones. From among them emerges first a tuft of leaves, which embrace one another, and make for a thick, striped stem below, like the leaves of *Curcuma Silvestris*,[5] but much larger, and not so smooth, a blackish green, deeply striped lengthwise, and full of folds, but in such a way, that some ridges commence in the center, sticking out sharply at the bottom, with other lesser ones among them, about four feet long, or more, one and a half to two hands wide, and each of the outside ones have their separate stem; they are thin, pointed in back and in front, and can be folded and bent any which way one likes. The young ones are somewhat hollow in their centers, like a little boat, but the old ones are expansive.

After the leaves one sees four or five pointed knobs near the roots, but above ground like a small Combilis,[6] divided into dark joints, like the purses of other Angreks, attached to the ground with many fibers. The flower-bearing stems appear to the sides of these knobs, four to five feet high, round, mostly bare, but slightly joined. On top they bear many purple flowers above one another, fashioned like Columbines.[7]

Each one is suspended from a longish little stem, and fashioned from five leaves, of which the three narrowest are spread out, of a light purple like Colchicum or Meadow Saffron.[8] In the center are two other, broader leaflets, slightly folded, on one side; with the others they cover another leaflet that is split in two on top, and that rests on a small yellow stem that is decorated with purple lines. To the sides grow yet two other, narrower leaflets, and in front of the same yet a third one, that is curved upwards above the aforementioned little stem, all a purplish red, and covered with the first two leaflets, without a main stem, fashioned like the bag below the neck of a pelican,[9] a mixture of purple and pale yellow; as soon as its flowers open, the stem becomes bellied and striped, and gradually turns into the fruit.

The latter is hexagonal, as with other Angreks, but with only three protruding ridges, and each one striped lengthwise with a groove, one and a half to two inches long, a finger thick, green, and it keeps the withered flower leaflets for a long time.

The ripe ones burst into three broader, and three narrower thongs, connected to each other in front and back as on an Imperial Crown;[10] inside is a yellowish meal, which turns gray, and drops out, leaving the little boats that contained the stems, which remain for a long time on the main stem, forming a separate cluster.

One will find a *second kind*,[11] which is held to be the female of the foregoing, very like it, except that the leaves are shorter, and only half the width; some are only three fingers wide, ridged lengthwise in the same fashion, full of folds, and fewer in number. The flower is the same, but smaller, totally white, or sometimes with a little purple below, also odorless. The purses near the roots are somewhat narrower and more pointed as well. If they grow in a rich clay soil, the purses of some of the first kind become so thick that they resemble the tubers[12] of Combilis, and sometimes one sees nothing else on this plant but these knobbles, four or five together, without leaves or stems, plantlike and fibrous inside, slimy at first, thereafter changing to a dry, spongy substance, as we mentioned above about the *Angraecum scriptum*.[13] But when planted in gardens it will not produce thick tubers.

Name. In Latin *Angraecum terrestre primum purpureum* and *album;*[14] in Malay *Daun Corra Corra*, after the shape of the leaf which, as I said, resembles the hold of a Karakar;[15] others call it with a common name *Angrec tana.*[16] The Ambonese call it *Ahaan*, a name it shares with the subsequent *Involucrum*,[17] because they consider both plants to be of the same kind.

Place. These plants have already abased themselves by coming

Tab. LII.

Cacopit

B

Fig. 2.

A

Fig. 1.

down out of the trees, and now grow on the ground, though they do not come down as far as the plains, for one will always find them in steep places, mostly in valleys, where the land has dropped away, and where on top grows only a tall grass, called *Hulong*.[18] The white kind is seldom found; one can find both on the steep banks of the *Alf* River,[19] where it sometimes can be obtained with great difficulty; they can also be transplanted into gardens, where it will take a year before they will bear flowers.

Use. These flowers are used only as an ornament; one ties them with the leaves around Saguer[20] pots, and they wrap all kinds of fruits in it, which are brought to market, as will be said about the subsequent Involucrum. The roots and leaves have a strange sharpness, that is somewhat like that of the Helleborus.

The picture shows a little bird near a flower, with a long, curved little beak, being a kind of Regulus or Kinglet, which is so small and light, that it can sit on all kinds of flowers, and sucks the sap or dew from them.[21]

The Fifty Second Plate.

The first Figure shows the *first Ground Angrek*,[22] showing its flower, A, separately, and the little bird called *Cacopit*. The *other Ground Angrek* is depicted in the *previous* Plate 50.[23] The second Figure[24] shows the *thrice-folded flower*, described in Chapter 13, with the *selfsame's fruit*, B, separately.

Chapter Eleven

THE SECOND GROUND ANGREK.

T he second kind of ground *Angrek,* has a rather thick, creeping root, almost like a Curcuma, that produces some thick stems, striped lengthwise with sharp ridges, and with transverse joints. The leaves also grow clasping one another, and resemble those of a young Pinang[1] sprout, or of *Helleborus albus,*[2] two and a half spans long, one and a half hand wide, divided lengthwise by five ridges, smooth, and a bright green.

One or two other straight and round stems come forth from the main stem, one and a half span long, whereon grow flowers above one another, the size of *Angrek primum.*

The flower has five white outer leaves, and inside a wide yellowish little helmet, its wings embracing the central triangular pillar, and both stand up straight under the top leaflet, being one of the aforementioned five, which also inclines over the flower like a little boat; the fruit grows behind the flower from the foot, being an oblong, hexagonal pod, green on the outside, with a yellowish meal inside, as in the first Angrek.

The main root looks like a piece of Curcuma,[3] and when

the leaves and old stem have dropped off it bulges from the ground, and it has other thick, long fibers at the sides, which crawl along the ground like worms.

Name. In Latin *Angraecum terrestre alterum;*[4] in Malay *Angrec tana.*[5]

Place. It creeps along flat ground, also on bald mountains, where there is a dell, and some thickets, as in flat valleys, in the grass along rivers, and can be easily transplanted into gardens.

Its *use* is still unknown, except that it does not have as sharp a taste as the foregoing, and is closer to the true Angrek.

N.B. This Ground Angrek was shown before in *fig. 3.* on *Plate 50.,*[6] and corresponds to Bela pola in the *H. Malab. part. 11. Tab. 35,*[7] which in *Commelin's Note*[8] was called the Indian, broad-leaved Gladiolus that grows in swamps, with a whitish flower, also in *Fl. Malab.*[9] p. 33. and by *Plukn.* in *Amalth.*[10] p. 106.

Chapter Twelve

THE WRAPPER.

*I*nvolucrum[1] is the third kind of *Angraecum terrestre;* its leaves resemble those of the first kind, for they are full of ridges and folds, at the back with sharp protruding ridges down its length, but finer than with the first one, thin, smooth, and of a blackish green, each one growing on a ridged stem, and clasping each other, like the Curcuma,[2] together with the stem some three to four feet long, two hands wide.

The flowers and fruits appear in a peculiar manner, not like an Angrek, but more like a Globba.[3] For a short spike[4] rises up from the roots from between the leaves, fashioned from dirty-green leaves or scales, like the Hypophyton[5] of the Globba durion[6] or Curcuma, but much smaller. Little hollow flowers peep from among the leaflets, divided into six points on top, yellow, that quickly wither. Thereafter one will see the spike, covered with long, dark-gray leaflets, and between them grow the fruits, which are round, oblong, green berries, like small rooster balls, with some dried flower leaflets on top. They are filled inside with black kernels, that are enveloped in a silvery slime or marrow, as one will see in the Globba, but without smell or taste.

It has a transverse root, an inch thick, spongy like Cork, with blackish spots and dots inside, on the outside enveloped by countless tiny fibers. The Hypophyton is seldom seen, hiding between the leaves, mostly in January.

Name. In Latin *Involucrum;* after the common Malay [name] *Daun bonkus,*[7] which means *Folium involutionis;* but the real Malay call it *Cattari;* others call it *Daun corra corra,* like the first kind, in Ambonese *Ahaain.*

Place. It grows in mountain forests, but in places where it is airy, and the trees are widely spaced, around rural roads for instance, where [the ground] is sharp and stony, or in red clay, where it is firmly rooted. It never grows by itself, but always in groups, though not attached to each other, and is not easily transplanted because of its wild nature.

Use. The Natives use it a great deal in their households, for they gather these leaves in the forests, and use them to wrap Kanari [nuts],[8] Lemons, and all sorts of fruits and fish, which they carry to market, or want to send to others, for these leaves are most suitable for this purpose because they have the shape of a boat, are tough, and come to a point both in back and in front, wherefore whatever is wrapped remains well covered. No Medicinal use is known.

Another plant that differs markedly from the foregoing is the one that is considered the male, which is why the Ambonese call it *Ahaain malona.* The leaves are much smaller and narrower, and so sharply ridged that it seems they have folds, disposed around a low trunk, a sad black-green, and covered at its place of origin with a prickly down or hair, as is the trunk or central

Tab. LIII.

stem, which emerges from the center, three feet high, round, stiff, and as thick as a goose quill, inside dry and hollow[9] with a thin plume on top, consisting of thin stems, and enveloped with a downy and almost sticky seed, which will stick very easily to one's hands and clothes, and makes your skin itch, as will the small gray hairs of the aforementioned stem.

It prefers to grow on river banks in the plains. It has no particular use, since it is difficult to handle because of the aforementioned hairs; the round stems are used to blow in somebody's eyes and ears, when something has fallen in one's eyes, and some dirt remains sticking in them, and the same thing with somebody's ears, when they hurt from a cold cathar.

If the one that was described first is in a shadowy place, it grows so tall, that one would think it was a different or large kind, for it grows to a length of at least six feet, and the leaf is easily three or four and a half feet long, seven inches wide, the rest below being a deeply grooved stem, and eight or ten of these leaves rise up from one root, that is as short as a small stump, draped with a host of thick, tough fibers.

It bears near the root two or three tufts as Cardamom[10] does, but smaller, with small yellow flowers, and after these come fruits that look like small cloves of Garlic, and these contain small, round, black, crackling seed, like Mustard, empty inside, and tasteless.

The Fifty Third Plate.

Shows the plant called the *Wrapper,* with its *Suckers,* and the *flower* and *fruit* separately.

Chapter Thirteen

THE TRIPLE FLOWER.

T he fourth kind[1] resembles *Helleborus albus*[2] or *Gentiana*[3] the most, and differs so much from the Angreks, that I prefer to consider it a singular plant, but the Natives regard it (as another) kind of Involucrum. It has three or four large leaves, which together make for a thick, angular stem, eighteen to twenty inches long, six wide, striped lengthwise with five ridges, that make a sharp edge below, as with Plantago,[4] otherwise smooth, thin, and a bright green.

It ends below in a thick stem, striped on the outside, and grooved inside. When [these leaves] begin to wither, the ridges are bared; a single stem rises up from the center of this congregation, the thickness of a quill, round, divided into a few dark joints, easily two feet tall, bearing few flowers on top.

These flowers have a particular shape, different from all the Angreks, because it seems as if three flowers grow above one another, all white, odorless, of which the lower part is fashioned from five leaflets, smaller and narrower than a Jasmine blossom, and the three larger ones are disposed in a triangle; the central one resembles a small helmet somewhat, and one can see something yellowish or mossy in its mouth, like fine threads with a tail, as with Larkspurs. The third and upper part, opposite the little helmet, has four leaflets, whereof the two center ones are curved away from one another, like the Astronomical sign Aries.[5]

Every flower has a rather long neck, and a green leaflet where it originates. After the flower has withered, the neck or stem begins to thicken, and forms a rather longish, striped, and angular pod, an inch long, like those of other Angreks, that hides small sandy seed, and if one opens the unripe pod, and rubs the seed between one's fingers, it will turn the color of lead.

The root is fashioned from many thick fibers, very like worms, bare when above ground, the color of smoke below, green on top, and with a tough sinew inside; the taste is insipid at first, but then turns quite sharp, like some Gentiana, burning the mouth, so that one's lips will swell, and one's throat gets hoarse, and one even feels this sharpness somewhat in the leaves, wherein it differs from all the Angreks. It blooms in October.

Name. In Latin *Flos triplicatus,*[6] or *Helleborus Amboinicus,*[7] in ordinary Malay *Bonga tiga lapis;*[8] the Ambonese consider it of the same kind as the foregoing *Involucrum,* and call it *Ahaan albal,* and *Ahaän Malona,* that is to say *wild* and *male Ahaän.*

Place. It grows in mountain forests, especially where much brush and dried leaves are piled up and are rotting. I have found it in the bright *Caju puti* forests,[9] and under the creeping fern *Filix calamaria,*[10] where there was a black and somewhat moist soil, covered with rotten leaves, its snake-like roots so loose above the ground, that one could easily pull it off, but it is seldom found.

After it has been transplanted into a garden, it takes its time before it decides whether it will grow or not, but when surrounded with its natural mountain soil and stones, it will produce its leaves and flowers, which will perish every year down to the root.

There is also a different kind, in terms of its leaves, though it grows like the foregoing; the flowers are also white, but not as clearly divided into three parts. The fruits are angular pods, somewhat longer than the foregoing, filled inside with a sandy meal.

Use. Since this entire plant is quite sharp, one should use it carefully for swollen hands (which is still little known), which is called *Hismi,* that is to say blessed or enchanted; one takes these roots with some Nutmeg, Bangle,[11] Tsjonker,[12] and Ginger, rub it all together, and tie it to the swelling.

The Natives have such tough mouths, that they dare to take these sharp roots internally, and chew it along with Pinang,[13] Nutmeg, and Ginger, against a persistent diarrhea caused by cold or raw dampness.

N.B. This plant's figure was shown before on *Tab.* 52. *fig.* 2.

Chapter Fourteen

THE LARGE AMBONESE ORCHIS.

Having discussed four kinds of Angrekum terrestre, which resemble Helleborine or Helleborus,[1] I will now present four others, which correspond to Orchis[2] or Standelwort,[3] wherefore they can also be thought of as Ambonese Orchides. The first and most handsome kind was described before, in Book 8, among garden herbs, under the name *Flos susanae*,[4] because it is such a close kin of *Amica nocturna*.[5]

The other three we will describe in two chapters, under the names *Orchis Amboinica Major* and *minor*.

This chapter includes two kinds of *Orchis major*, the first one with a branched root, the other with one that looks like a Radish.

I. *Orchis Amboinica major, radice digitata*,[6] has only one or two leaves, that look a great deal like those of the foregoing *Daun corra corra*,[7] but they are much narrower, two and a half or three feet long, two inches wide, pointed on top and bottom, standing there like little swords, also ridged lengthwise with five sinews and folds. It has the most leaves in January, thereafter a single bare stem which is also two and a half feet tall, bearing few flowers on top, like normal Angreks, fashioned of five leaflets with a short little bag, whitish, with purple stripes, but the little helmet has purple drops.

The fruit is an oblong pod like a finger, and barely that thick, a dark green, striped with ridges lengthwise, with a yellowish meal inside.

The root resembles the root of *Lampujang*[8] or *Ginger*, for it grows aslant in the ground like a clump of many fingers or claws, whereof two or three hang together, with narrow necks like Calbahaar puti.[9]

It is whitish on the outside, and semi transparent when held against the light of a candle, filled with a tough slime, bitter and unpleasant, with a smell like a dog.

II. *Orchis Amboinica major, radice Raphanoide*,[10] has five or six leaves that close together very near the root, and are even narrower than the foregoing, two feet long, barely a finger wide, and finely ridged, so that one could hold it to be a reed. The flowers appear from the center of the leaves, just above the root in a sheath, each one on a short stem, one or two, a dirty white, mixed with some light red, like those of Tommon cantsje.[11] Below each flower is an oblong, striped little purse, that contains an angular, black seed.

The root goes straight down into the earth, like a small Radish, easily a finger long, and thick, or less, blackish on the outside, white inside and slimy like the foregoing, draped with thick fibers like Ginger, leaving little black stipples behind when it is peeled. The taste comes close to that of Satyrium,[12] not bitter, but cloying, and a little sharp.

Name. Orchis Amboinica major; the first kind, *Radice digitata;* the other, *Radice raphanoide;* I do not know of any special name in Malay, only the common *Angrek tana;*[13] the first one could be called *Angrek tana alea;*[14] due to its Ginger-shaped root. The second [could be called] *Angrek tana itam,*[15] because of its black root. It has no name in Ambonese. On Ternate it is called *Panawa Sassiri-isso* because of the following use.

Place. Both grow on bare and cool[16] mountains, and high plains, under Carex or Hulong grass.[17] They grow a lot on bald mountains near Victoria Castle. One does not see them throughout the year, only around January, but only if they bear flowers, for its narrow leaves are otherwise difficult to distinguish from Carex grass, and one will often find, that the sharp tips, which this grass shoots up from the root, penetrate like awls through the root of the first kind, growing right through it. It is a strange sight to see one plant grow through the root of another one, and those tips of that grass are so penetrating, that one will often find them growing through much thicker roots, like Ubi[18] and Combily.[19]

Use. The first root looks the most like Satyrium; they can be candied, but they first have to be drained, when they become as clear as Amber,[20] but it remains very tough and hairy when it is chewed, and keeps some of its nasty smell. But it finally falls apart in one's mouth, and one should always choose the youngest ones, to wit, those that are the whitest on that clump, or that are the first to bear flowers. The second root, that looks like a radish, is much better for this, since it has less of that nasty smell, and crumbles when chewed, almost melt-

Tab. LIV.

Fig. 1.
Spec. 2.

Fig. 3.

Fig. 2.

ing in one's mouth, and is considered to have the same effects as our European Satyria.

The Ternatans use the first root as a remedy against Abscesses,[21] called *Sassiri-isso,* which are big, blueish, causing little pain, but generating a great deal of pus. For they call large, red, hot swellings, such as bloody ulcers and boils,[22] *Sassiri-bara.* They take the root, crush it, wrap it in a leaf of *Buro malacco,* which is *Oculus astaci,*[23] heat it over a fire, and put it like that over the aforementioned Abscesses.

The Fifty Fourth Plate.

The first Figure[24] shows the *second kind* of the *great Ambonese Orchis.* The second Figure[25] indicates the *small Ambonese Orchis,* to wit the *first kind.*

The third Figure[26] represents the *second kind* of the *small Orchis.*

THE SMALL AMBONESE ORCHIS.

The fourth kind[1] is also a true Orchis, but smaller than all the foregoing ones.

It first produces long leaves, numbering three or four, shaped like grass, six to seven inches long, half a finger wide, thickish, and smooth, somewhat folded, and with a groove in the center; these wilt quickly, and from their midst emerges a single stem, whereon the leaves are disposed not over against but above each other, of unequal size; the lower ones are only a thumb joint long, and partially dried up, whereafter follow three or four longer ones, four to six inches long, broad, and grooved as before, with a long stiff tip. These are gradually followed by smaller ones, that lie close to the stem.

It bears a thick, short ear[2] on top, that has many white little flowers closely packed together, quite the same shape as our ordinary Orchis, except that they lack the sacks in the back; otherwise they gape in front, and have two tiny leaflets on top, like two little wings, a curved little horn towards the front, and with a long little beard below, curved backwards, altogether white; the flowers on the top part of this ear are usually closed.

The fruits are small, angular pods, with a slimy meal inside, but few reach perfection. The root is very small, and short,[3] to wit, white, short and thickish fibers, and at the bottom hang usually two, seldom one, oblong glands, like testicles, of which one is usually small and more wrinkled, gray on the outside, inside white and sappy, slimy, and with a sweetish taste, almost like cooked Combilis.[4]

It flowers at the end of the rainy season, and in the beginning of the dry Monsoon,[5] and after it flowers the entire stem perishes, so that one will not find it again. Only the top fibers remain when it is pulled out of the ground. For the long glands are rather firmly stuck in the ground, which is why one should dig them up.

Name. In Latin *Orchis Amboinica minor;*[6] it has no name in Malay or Ambonese, or one should call it *Angrek kitsjil.*[7]

Place. Like the foregoing, it grows on airy hills, and also on plains among Carex grass,[8] and one will hardly notice it there unless it has flowers. One always finds many of them together where the grass is lower and shorter, as on the red mountain[9] near Victoria Castle, where the entire troop blooms at the same time, and they also perish together. It loves a black, hard clay soil, and if one wants to transplant it, one should dig up the root after flowering, clean it of the fibers, keep it dry for several days, and then transplant it in the same kind of soil, but it likes to be elevated, and does not like shady or moist places.

Use. It is unknown to the Natives, but I have found it to be better and tastier for candying than the foregoing, because when candied it is crumbly, crunchy, and sweet in the mouth, and without that nasty smell. But it is difficult to find and dig up because the roots are at their best before they flower, which is when they are hard to find in that grass, and I had them dig in the same place where the plant perished, but could not find any roots that looked like those glands, so one can say that it shoots up suddenly, and vanishes just as suddenly.

A second kind[10] becomes slightly taller, to wit, three to four spans[11] high, shooting up with a single, round stem, that is bare about two hands[12] above the root, whereafter one will find a congregation of five to six leaflets above one another, on the main stem without a foot, like those of the Angrek, four inches long, two fingers[13] wide, striped lengthwise with five ridges, of which the central one protrudes below, and makes for a groove on top; the other four are dark, and protrude more on top, whereafter the main stem continues bare again, and makes a long ear, easily a span long, densely covered with little flowerlets, hollow, like those of the *Herba supplex*,[14] divided into five tips, a whitish yellow, followed by the fruits, a fingernail long, mostly triangular, filled inside with a slimy meal, like the other Angreks, and scentless.

The root consists of two little balls, of which the largest is as long as one's little finger, the thickness of a finger, usually sticking out to the side; the other one is much smaller and thinner, right below the stalk, draped with few fibers, mostly under the trunk,[15] russet on the outside, inside white and watery.

This concludes the plants that are considered Angreks.

Comment.

Mr. *Breyne*'s *Centuria*[16] has several handsome varieties of Orchis, and the second kind of the small Orchis corresponds to the taller and broad-leaved Orchis, with the Asphodil root, and a rigid, narrow ear in *Sloan. Cat. pl. p. 119.*[17] and *Jam. Hist. part one Tab. 147. fig. 2.*[18] Basaala poulou Marabara, in *H. Malab. vol. 12. Tab. 27,*[19] belongs here as well.

THE SUSANNA FLOWER

*F*los Susannae[1] is an Ambonese *Orchis*[2] that can be put in the fourth Class of *Orchides,* called *Orchis Serapias,* as described by *Dodonaeus, lib. 7. cap. 30.*[3]

It shoots up with a single, straight, round, and firm stem 2 1/2 feet tall, whereof the lower part has few leaves, like those of the Plantain,[4] though longer, thicker, and smoother, six inches long, 2 fingers wide, lengthwise divided by 3 or 4 sinews, of which the middle one protrudes on the bottom with a sharp ridge, though the others do not stick out on the bottom.

These leaves embrace the main stem and are sometimes widest at the top and sometimes at the bottom, and they are at their biggest and most luxurious before the stem shoots up, which then puts forth only a few other leaves, which are smaller and narrower than the former ones, snug against the stem, viscous and unpleasant to the taste.

Four or five entirely white flowers appear at the top of the stem, a blend of singular and rare shapes, like both an Iris and an Orchid, but as large as the largest Narcissus, for each flower is made up of 6 large leaflets of which two are a dirty white and curve backwards; the third, being the largest, stands up straight, bends forward a little and over the flower, resting within on two white and pronged little horns. The other two, wider than the others, cover the borders, and their outer edges are cut into many rays, as if they were fringed.

Between these two lies the sixth, lowest and smallest leaflet, folded together like a little boat. In the center one sees a hollow leaflet, shaped like a little Helmet, with two thin little horns on the side that curve back upon themselves towards the inside, and hide under the little helmet, bearing yellow Buds, as in white Lilies. Behind this little helmet one sees two white and gleaming hillocks or glands, with a hole beneath them that goes all the way to the stem. The flower has a long and somewhat crooked tail at the back, hanging down for some 6 inches, as thick as an oaten pipe, round, hollow inside, on the outside green and white.

The foot of the flower is an angular and green stem, with edges that are sharp and sawed, two inches long, fairly thick in the middle, and sprouting from the lap of a small leaf on the main stem. This foot becomes the fruit, being an oblong pod the length of a finger joint, more than the thickness of a quill, divided by six sharp edges, containing a hairy and russet-like wool instead of seeds, as in the Angrecis,[5] that flies out and disperses when the ripe pods burst at the sides into six narrow strips which are still linked together at their tips. The smell is sweet, like that of a Lily, but faint.

At first I could not find a true root, for the end of the main stem became a little stump in the ground, with a few short fibers hanging from it. And at the time there were also few leaves to be seen on it, as all *Orchides* are wont to do when they bear flowers. But at other times, when it is not bearing flowers yet, one will find perfect glandulous roots, to wit, an oblong little globe, like a Testicle, somewhat uneven and lying slant-wise, and with one or, more rarely, with 2 lesser ones, as if dried out, on each side. These Testicles are often of the same size, but one will always be more wrinkled, and spongier and slightly smaller, as is true of all Orchids. The taste is watery, insipid, and somewhat bitter, as with all Satyria.

One sees these flowers rarely, mostly in the rainy months of June and July, because at other times it loses its stem and leaves, though I have found them in December; in any case, they are not often found on Amboina, and only during the rainy season.

Name. Since I have not been able to find either a Malay or an Ambonese name, I call it *Flos Susannae* in Latin. In Malay: *Bonga*[6] Susanna, in memory of her[7] who when alive, was my first Companion and Helpmate in looking for herbs and plants, and who was also the first one to show it to me. Some would want to call it an *Angrec tana*[8] in Malay, but that name belongs properly to another plant.

Place. One finds it in Leytimor[9] in the mountains, near Fort Victoria, to the East, especially on the road to Rietton, under low bushes, and where *Caju Puti* trees[10] grow.

When dug up before its stem has appeared, it can be transplanted to gardens, where it will produce its flower and show it fully opened for days on end, and the Year next will fashion a new plant again. But if transplanted when the flower has opened already, it will not want to bloom and will perish in the earth.

Use. Of its virtues and use nothing is known up till now, unless that it is a handsome and rare flower because of its wondrous shape, worthy of being planted in pots and flower beds.

Maccabuhay[11] is perhaps a similar flower and root that grows in Manilha, and its root is candied there by the Chinese, wherefore I too had the Ambonese one dug up when the roots were the largest, that is before the flowers appear, and had them cleaned and soaked in water for several days until they lost their nasty and bitter taste, and then boiled them with sugar, but I found that cooking made them hard, and when chewing them they were like gristle, and grainy, but tasted better after a Year.

There is also a smaller kind[12] of *Flos Susannae,* no more than a foot high, with similar leaves and glands, but both much smaller.

The flower is very small, also white and finely notched, but otherwise like the larger one. It is seldom found, and then only on windy mountains; its Testicles are larger and more noticeable than the former one, also more fit to be candied, though they should be dug up before they flower, even if they are then more difficult to find because the little leaves are scarcely to be distinguished from young grass, and after the flower has perished one will not find a single leaf.

The *Satyria* are also found in China, and are called *Pu Sang-Tjan*[13] there, which means: mother without a child, or child without a mother, because the leaves of the plant have with-

Tab. XCIX.

Fig. 1.

Fig. 2.

Fig. 2.

Fig. 3.

ered when the flower-bearing stem is in bloom, as one can also see in Europe. They rub the roots in vinegar and smear it on certain white spots on the face.

The Ninety Ninth Plate.

The *first Figure* shows a small young plant of the *Susanne flower*, before it has flowered.

The *second Figure* indicates a perfect flower-bearing plant of the *Susanne flower*, with its stem divided in two because of its height.

The *third Figure* shows only the top part of the stem with fruits, after its leaves have already withered and dropped off.

Comment.

Anyone can clearly see that this plant is a true kind of *Orchis*, with exceptional flowers, and a particularly long tail, and it was called the Ambonese *Orchis* with white fringed flowers; Rumphius' *Susanne flower* can be found in *Herman*,[14] in his *Par. Bat. Pr. p.* 358, while added to the one in *Plukenet's Mantissa*,[15] *p.* 141, was the beautiful fingered *Orchis*, with flowers of the mountain Clove tree, the edges as if fringed, from Virginia, &c.

THE PETOLA LEAF.

We will close the tenth book with this masterpiece of nature,[1] being a small low little plant, consisting of few leaves, but these are beautifully painted, as if wrought by art; it has a single, weak stem, not more than two or three inches high, so that this little plant is almost lying on the ground. It has three leaves on top, spread out in what is almost a triangle, and below them another two or three smaller ones, which divide the stem somewhat into joints, and cover it partly with their sheaths, like the leaves of *Alsine Indica* or *Arundinella*,[2] a family to which it appears to belong.[3]

The larger leaflets also resemble *Arundinella latifolia*[4] somewhat, but shorter, and rounder, some are also a bit heart-shaped, thickish, but limp. It is chestnut brown on the upper side, perhaps darker, soft to the touch, like plush, and somewhat shiny, very handsomely painted, with light-red or yellow lines, that run through one another, representing small squares, or unknown characters, as if a skilled Painter had limned them with a fine brush. The leaves are red on the under side, the color purple, without characters. And so it stands there for a long time, without showing anything else but these three or four painted leaflets.

Finally it produces a single soft stem from its center, round, woolly, five to six inches tall, divided into three or four dark joints, whereon appear some little white flowers, that soon perish, and beneath them the little stem begins to thicken, and forms a triangular fruit, like that of *Empetrum acetosum*,[5] to wit, an oblong little house, fashioned from three little fleeces or wings, but more oblong than that of *Empetrum*, a mixed color of green and brown, keeping the withered little flower for a long time on top.

This pod finally splits into three parts, but remains attached on top and bottom, and then a fine seed falls out, similar to that of *Empetrum*, leaving three bare little threads between the thongs.

The root is small, fashioned from few, thick, and white fibers, weakly fixed to the ground, for it grows always in a loose and moist soil.

Name. In Latin *Folium petolatum*,[6] after the Malay *Daun petola*, because it resembles a rich silk cloth, called *Petola*,[7] that has been painted with many colors.

Place. It is rarely found, hence it is not known to most Natives. It always grows on tall, remote mountains, where tall trees provide shade, but are widely spaced,[8] and the soil beneath them is somewhat moist. I have taken a great deal of trouble to transplant it into gardens, and it did grow for quite a while, but perished each time without producing seed. The Ambo-

Tab. XLI.

Fig. 1.

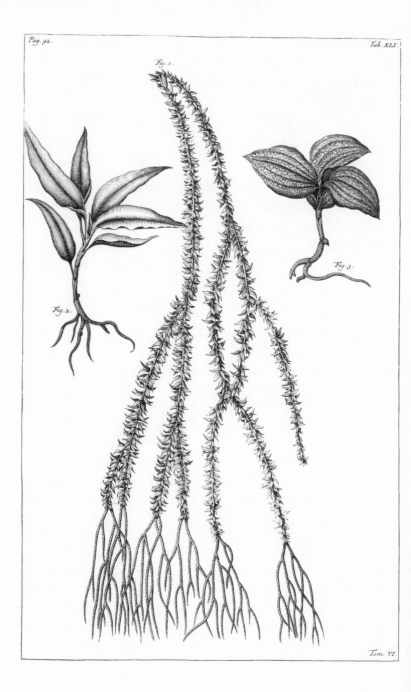

Fig. 2.

Fig. 3.

nese have better luck sometimes, when they transplant it into their mountain plots.

Use. None is known, so that it is only displayed as a curiosity that has come down from the mountains. I was unable to depict it with either pen or brush, because the lineaments on the leaves were too ingenious, wherefore I pasted the entire plant here on a piece of paper, all the more so, because dried it preserves its colors better.[9]

The Forty First Plate.

Shows in the first Figure a *scaled Equiseet* that *grows on trees,* and that is also called the *Horse Tail.*

The second Figure indicates the *Pethola leaf,* which is called *the Male.*

The third Figure depicts the *Pethola leaf* or the *Female,* or the *real one,* both of which are described in [this] Chapter.

ABBREVIATIONS

ACC	Georgius Everhardus Rumphius, *The Ambonese Curiosity Cabinet.* Translated, edited, annotated, and with an introduction by E. M. Beekman. New Haven: Yale University Press, 1999.
Chen	Chen Sing-Chi and Tang Tsin, "A General Review of the Orchid Flora of China." *Orchid Biology. Reviews and Perspectives, II,* ed. Joseph Arditti. Ithaca, N.Y.: Cornell University Press, 1982.
Comber	J. B. Comber, *Orchids of Java.* London: Royal Botanic Gardens, Kew, 1990.
De Clercq	F. S. A. De Clercq, *Nieuw Plantkundig Woordenboek voor Nederlandsch Indië* 2d rev. ed. Amsterdam: J. H. de Bussy, 1927.
De Haan	F. de Haan, *Priangan. De Preanger-Regentschappen onder het Nederlandsch Bestuur tot 1811.* 4 vols. Batavia: Bataviaasch Genootschap van Kunsten en Wetenschappen, 1910–1912.
De Wit	H. D. C. de Wit, "Orchids in Rumphius' *Herbarium Amboinense.*" In *Orchid Biology: Reviews and Perspectives, I,* ed. Joseph Arditti. Ithaca, N.Y.: Cornell University Press, 1977. Pp. 48–94.
Dressler	Robert L. Dressler, *The Orchids: Natural History and Classification.* 1981. Reprint ed., Cambridge: Harvard University Press, 1990.

G   *Rumphius Gedenkboek 1702–1902.* Ed. M. Greshoff.
                    Haarlem: Koloniaal Museum, 1902.

Gerard   John Gerard, *The Herbal or General History of Plants*
                    [1633]. Revised and enlarged by Thomas Johnson.
                    Reprint ed., New York: Dover, 1975.

Heniger   J. Heniger, *Hendrik Adriaan van Reede tot Drakenstein*
                    (1636–1691) and Hortus Malabaricus: A Contribution to
                    the History of Dutch Colonial Botany. Rotterdam: A. A.
                    Balkema, 1986.

Heyne   K. Heyne, *De Nuttige Planten van Nederlandsch Indië.*
                    2d rev. ed., 2 vols. Batavia: Department van Land-
                    bouw, Nijverheid & Handel in Nederlandsch-
                    Indië, 1927.

Jacquet   Pierre Jacquet, "History of Orchids in Europe,
                    from Antiquity to the 17th Century." In *Orchid*
                    Biology: Reviews and Perspectives, VI, ed. Joseph Arditti.
                    New York: John Wiley, 1994. Pp. 33–102.

Lawler   Leonard J. Lawler, "Ethnobotany of the Orchida-
                    ceae." In *Orchid Biology. Reviews and Perspectives, III,* ed.
                    Joseph Arditti. Ithaca, N.Y.: Cornell University
                    Press, 1984. Pp. 27–149.

Leupe   P. A. Leupe, "Georgius Everardus Rumphius,
                    Ambonsch Natuurkundige der zeventiende eeuw."
                    Verhandelingen der Koninklijke Akademie van Wetenschappen,
                    vol. XII. Amsterdam: C. G. van der Post, 1871. Pp.
                    1–63.

Lewis & Short   Charlton T. Lewis and Charles Short, *A Latin*
                    Dictionary. Oxford: Clarendon Press, 1879.

M   E. D. Merrill, *An Interpretation of Rumphius's Her-*
                    barium Amboinense. Manila: Bureau of Printing,
                    1917.

MV   *Rumphius Memorial Volume.* Ed. H. C. D. de Wit.
                    Baarn: Hollandia, 1959.

OED   *Oxford English Dictionary.* 17 vols. Oxford: Oxford
                 University Press, 1933.

Pliny   Pliny, *Natural History.* Trans. H. Rackham, W. H. S.
                 Jones, and D. E. Eichholz. 10 vols. Loeb Classical
                 Library. Cambridge: Harvard University Press,
                 1938–1962.

Reinikka   Merle Reinikka, *A History of the Orchid.* Coral
                 Gables, Fla.: University of Miami Press, 1972.

Smith   J. J. Smith, *Die Orchideen von Ambon.* Batavia:
                 Landsdrukkerij, 1905.

Valentijn   François Valentijn, *Oud en Nieuw Oost-Indiën.*
                 5 books in 8 volumes. Dordrecht and Amsterdam,
                 1724–1726.

Wilkinson   R. J. Wilkinson, *A Malay-English Dictionary (Roman-
                 ised).* 2 vols. Reprint ed., London: Macmillan,
                 1959.

WNT   *Woordenboek der Nederlandsche Taal.* 29 vols. The
                 Hague: Martinus Nijhoff & SDU Uitgeverij,
                 1882–1998.

Yule   Henry Yule and A. C. Burnell, *Hobson-Jobson: being
                 a Glossary of Anglo-Indian colloquial words and phrases*
                 [1886]. Reprint ed., New Delhi: Munshiram
                 Manoharlal, 1979.

NOTES

Introduction

1. Hansen, *Orchid Fever*, pp. 58 and 31. See also Orlean, *Orchid Thief*; Orlean cites $10 billion on p. 51.

2. Reinikka, *A History of the Orchid*, pp. 23–24; hereafter referred to as Reinikka, with page number(s). Reinikka's book is the only history of the movers and shakers of orchid history. Rumphius is not included.

3. The neologism is part of the private language shared by Swann and his mistress Odette in the first volume of Proust's *A la Recherche du Temps Perdu*, which is *Du Côté de chez Swann*, first published in 1913. The relevant passage reads in part: "... la métaphore 'faire catleya', devenue un simple vocable qu'ils employaient sans y penser quand ils voulaient signifier l'acte de la possession physique. . . ." See the Pléiade edition of this masterpiece: Proust, *A la Recherche du Temps Perdu*, 1:234.

4. There is ample evidence in Hansen, *Orchid Fever*, and Orlean, *Orchid Thief*.

5. Chase, Freudenstein, and Cameron, "DNA data and Orchidaceae Systematics," in *The First International Orchid Conservation Congress*, p. 22. See also Jacquet, "History of Orchids in Europe, from Antiquity to the 17th Century," in *Orchid Biology, VI*, p. 35; hereafter referred to as Jacquet, with page number(s). See also Lawler, "Ethnobotany of the Orchidaceae," in *Orchid Biology, III*, pp. 27–149; hereafter referred to as Lawler, with page number(s). For more detailed discussion of geographical data see Dressler, *The Orchids: Natural History and Classification*, pp. 14 ff.; hereafter referred to as Dressler, with page number(s). I

want to mention here that the series *Orchid Biology: Reviews and Perspectives*, edited by Joseph Arditti, now counting eight volumes, published by various publishers between 1977 and 2001, is probably the best mine of information for both specialist and general reader.

6. Dressler, p. 8.

7. See Jacquet.

8. *Woordenboek der Nederlandsche Taal* (hereafter *WNT*), vol. XV, under "standelkruid." There are 35 genera of European orchids, divided into 116 species. See *Flora Europea*, vol. 5: *Alismataceae to Orchidaceae (Monocotyledones)*, p. 35.

9. Chen Sing-Chi and Tang Tsin, "A General Review of the Orchid Flora of China" in *Orchid Biology, II*, p. 41; hereafter referred to as Chen, with page number(s). See also Needham, *Science and Civilisation in China*, vol. 6: *Biology and Biological Technology*, Part I: Botany, pp. 417–419.

10. In this famous passage from Chandler's superlative novel, orchids in a greenhouse are described as follows: "The plants filled the place, a forest of them, with nasty meaty leaves and stalks like the newly washed fingers of dead men. They smelled as overpowering as boiling alcohol under a blanket" (Chandler, *Stories and Early Novels*, p. 592). A good survey of the role of orchids in literature is Lewis, "Power and Passion: The Orchid in Literature" in *Orchid Biology, V*, pp. 207–249.

11. Dressler, p. 10; see also p. 8.

12. See ibid., p. 12, fig. 2.2.

13. Ordoño, *Diccionario de la Lengua Nahuatl.*

14. Lawler, p. 53.

15. Ibid., p. 54.

16. Reinikka, pp. 17–18.

17. Chen, p. 72. The breakdown of this total as given there is: "82 genera and 550 species are terrestrials, and 64 genera and 416 species are epiphytes. The remaining 17 genera and 33 species are 'saprophytes'." A saprophyte does not make its own food via photosynthesis, but avails itself of nourishment produced by other plants.

18. Ibid., p. 73.

19. Comber, *Orchids of Java*, p. 2; hereafter referred to as Comber, with page number(s).

20. Personal communication from Mr. Comber by letter, dated October 16, 2000.

21. Millar, *Orchids of Papua New Guinea*, pp. 3 and 8.

22. Smith, *Die Orchideen von Ambon*, pp. 4–5; hereafter referred to as Smith, with page number(s).

23. De Wit has 36 species, with 28 specific ones: De Wit, "Orchids in Rumphius' *Herbarium Amboinense*," in *Orchid Biology, I*, pp. 48–94; hereafter referred to as De Wit, with page number(s). J. B. Comber informed me by letter (January 8, 2001) that he also believes the total is 36, "but just how many of these are accurately named is open to interpretation. . . . Out of the 36 species mentioned, five have so far not been named to species level."

24. Reinikka, p. 16.

25. See my nn. 42–56 in ch. 1 for more detail.

26. This and other new information about Rumphius is based on original research and can be perused in more detail in the fully documented and longer introduction to my edition of Rumphius' other classic: *The Ambonese Curiosity Cabinet*, pp. xxxv–cxii. That volume is throughout this text referred to as *ACC*, with page number(s).

27. The poem is entitled "Georgii Everhardi Rumphii Peregrinatio, sive iter in Brasiliam," is 218 lines long, and was printed inexplicably after the title page of the sixth volume of his *Herbal*. See n. 32.

28. Valentini, *Museum Museorum*, p. 53.

29. Georgius Everhardus Rumphius, *De Ambonese Historie. Behelsende Een kort Verhaal der Gedenkwaardigste Geschiedenissen zo in Vreede als oorlog voorgevallen sedert dat de Nederlandsche Oost Indische Comp: Het Besit in Amboina Gehadt Heeft* [The History of Ambon. Containing a short Relation of the most Memorable Events that took place both in Peace and war since the Dutch East Indies Company took Possession of Amboina]. Published in the journal *Bijdragen tot de Taal-, Land- en Volkenkunde van Nederlandsch-Indië*, zevende volgreeks: tiende deel [vol. 64] (The Hague: Nijhoff, 1910), pp. 12 and 99.

30. The original reads: "quam ego, plus consuens, totum mundum cum omnibus creaturis subito meo visui subtraxit, unde jam per decennium in tristibus tenebris sedere cogor." Printed in *Miscellanea Curiosa sive Ephemeridum Medico-Physicarum Germanicarum Academiae Imperialis Leopoldinae Naturae Curiosorum.* (Nuremberg: Wolfgang Maurit Endter, 1683), p. 51. This publication printed Rumphius' thirteen Asian notices during his lifetime.

31. Leupe, "Georgius Everardus Rumphius," in *Verhandelingen der Koninklijke Akademie*, pp. 17–18; hereafter referred to as Leupe, with page number(s).

32. *Het Amboinsche Kruid-boek. Dat is, Beschryving van de meest bekende Boomen, Heesters, Kruiden, Land- en Water-Planten, die men in Amboina, en de omleggende eylanden vind, Na haare gedaante, verscheide benamingen, aanqueking, en gebruik: mitsgaders van eenige insecten en gediertens, Voor 't meeste deel met de Figuren daar toe behoorende, Allen met veel moeite en vleit in veele jaaren vergadert, en beschreven in twaalf boeken, door Georgius Everhardus Rumphius, Med. Doct. van Hanau, Oud Koopman en Raadspersoon in Amboina, mitsgaders onder de naam van Plinius Indicus, Lid van de Illustre Academia Naturae Curiosorum, in 't Duitsche en Roomsche Ryk opgerigt. Nagezien en uitgegeven door Joannes Burmannus, Med. Doct. en Botanices Professor in den Hortus Medicus te Amsterdam, Medelidt van het Keyzerlyke Queekschool der onderzoekers van de Natuurkunde; Die daar verscheide Benamingen, en zyne Aanmerkingen heeft bygevoegt*, 6 vols. (Amsterdam, By François Changuion, Jan Catuffe, Hermanus Uytwerf; In 's Hage, By Pieter Gosse, Jean Neaulme, Adriaan Moetjens, Antony van Dole; Te Utrecht, By Steven Neaulme, 1741–1750). The Utrecht publisher did not participate in producing volumes 5 and 6. One should mention that the main title is variously printed as *"Amboinsch Kruid-boek," "Kruyd-boek," "Kruydboek,"* and *"Kruidboek."* I use *"Amboinsche Kruidboek,"* just *"Kruidboek,"* or *"Herbal."* As far as we know, Rumphius did not earn a degree in medicine, nor is this distinction mentioned on the title page of *D'Amboinsche Rariteitkamer.* The complete title of the "Auctuarium" or volume 7 is: *Het Auctuarium, ofte Vermeerdering, op het Amboinsch Kruyd-boek. Dat is, Beschryving van de overige Boomen, Heesters, en Planten, die men in Amboina, en de omleggende eilanden vind, Allen zeer accuraat beschreven en afgebeeldt na der zelver gedaantes, met*

*de verscheide Indische benamingen, aanqueking, en gebruik, door Georgius Everhardus
Rumphius, Med. Doct. van Hanau, Oud Koopman en Raadspersoon in Amboina,
mitsgaders onder de naam van Plinius Indicus, Lid van de Illustre Academia Naturae
Curiosorum, in't Duitsche en Roomsche Ryk opgerigt. Nu voor 't eerst uitgegeven, en in
het Latyn overgezet, door Joannes Burmannus, Med. Doctor, en Botanices Professor in
het Illustre Athenaeum, en de Hortus Medicus te Amsteldam, Medelidt van het Keizerlyke Queekschool der onderzoekers van de Natuurkunde; Die daar verscheide Benamingen, en zyn Aanmerkingen heeft bygevoegt* (Amsterdam, By Mynard Uytwerf, en de Wed. S. Schouten en Zoon, 1755). [The Auctuarium, or
Addition, to the Ambonese Herbal. That is, Description of the remaining Trees, Shrubs, and Plants, which are found in Amboina, and
the surrounding islands, All very accurately described and depicted according to their proper shapes, with their various Indian names, cultivations, and use, by Georgius Everhardus Rumphius, Med. Doct. from
Hanau, Former Merchant and Counselor in Amboina, also known by
the name of Plinius Indicus, Member of the Illustre Academia Naturae Curiosorum, founded in the Holy Roman Empire. Now published
for the first time, and translated into Latin, by Johannes Burmannus,
Med. Doctor, and Professor of Botany at the Illustre Athenaeum, and
the Hortus Medicus in Amsterdam, Fellow member of the Imperial
Academy of inquirers into Nature; Who has added various Names,
and his Comments.] Hereafter references to *Het Amboinsche Kruidboek* or
The Ambonese Herbal will be given in the text between brackets, by volume
number and page(s): i.e., 2:241.

33. Merrill, *An Interpretation of Rumphius's Herbarium Amboinense*, p. 14;
hereafter referred to as M, with page number(s).

34. M, p. 30.

35. M, p. 12.

36. Van de Wetering, *Rembrandt*, pp. 60–69, esp. p. 67.

37. Ibid., p. 69.

38. Dressler, p. 313. For Rumphian "firsts" in terms of orchids see
also De Wit, pp. 48–94.

39. See Wehner, Zierau, and Arditti, "Plinius Germanicus and Plinius Indicus," in *Orchid Biology, VIII*, pp. 1–81.

40. See ch. 1.

41. Reinikka, p. 17.

42. Comber, p. 306.

43. The composite name for this orchid genus is derived from the Greek φαλλαινα a word for a moth, specifically a species they called "flying soul" (πετομένη ψυχή and ὄψις which means "the aspect of [something]").

44. Comber, p. 305.

45. De Wit, p. 94.

Chapter One

1. Original text in 11.1.6:95–100.

A fine example of Rumphius' wit. His readers did not know what epiphytes were, so this is an elegant way to present the main division of these plants: epiphytic and terrestrial orchids. The metaphor includes a sly dig at aristocrats, a social species with which Rumphius was well acquainted and which he did not like (see the introduction). The remark about castles and fortresses is based on personal experience. Rumphius' ancestral region, the Wetterau, had a number of these keeps built in high places to make them unassailable. His father was a fortifications expert and had passed the skill on to his son. Finally, Rumphius knew of sudden reversals of aristocratic fortune during the Thirty Years War. It had happened to a member of the Solms clan, a family of local nobility who were his father's employers.

2. "Helleborine" means a "plant like hellebore," which is rather confusing; hellebore (genus *Helleborus*) is a species of the Ranunculaceae. It was a fabled plant used for medicinal purposes, especially to treat mental disease. Helleborine was once considered a separate genus of orchids, but is today regarded as a species of orchid either of the genus *Cephalanthera* or of Epipactis (the latter was formerly known as Serapias, a name Rumphius uses as well). Rumphius appears to be employing it as a generic term for orchid species.

3. *Calceolaria* is a large genus of tropical American plants of the family Scrophulariaceae, which have little to do with orchids.

Although Rumphius, once again, seems to use the phrase rather generically, "Calceolus mariae" was also the name in the herbals (for instance Gerard, *The Herbal or General History of Plants*, p. 443; hereafter Gerard, with page number[s]), for the lovely Lady's Slipper, a temperate-zone orchid of the genus *Cypripedium*. The latter compound noun literally means "Venus' Slippers" while the word "Lady" in our vernacular name referred originally to the Virgin Mary. "Calceolus" is Latin for a "small shoe."

4. There are an estimated 25,000 species of orchids on earth, of which Indonesia has more than 5,000, many of them unique.

5. Merrill (M, p. 177) lists it as *Grammatophyllum scriptum* (L.).

The Dutch botanist Joannes Jacobus Smith contributed the section on Rumphius' orchids in Merrill's *Interpretation of Rumphius's Herbarium Amboinense*. Hence all identifications here are by Smith, not Merrill. Smith based his assessments on his previous monograph, *Die Orchideen von Ambon*.

Smith was born in Antwerp in 1867 and died in Oegstgeest in 1947. For most of his professional life he worked for the Botanic Gardens in Bogor (then Buitenzorg) on Java, becoming its director from 1913 to 1924. He traveled extensively in Java but also took part in lengthy botanical expeditions to the Moluccas (including Ambon) and Celebes (Sulawesi). Though he published papers on a number of plants, he is especially remembered as an orchidologist.

Rumphius' original name is a hybrid, since "angraecum" is a Latinized form of the Javanese *anggrèk*, a noun that is still the general Indonesian word for "orchid." "Scriptum" means inscribed, written upon.

6. "Maare-takken" in the original. This is the Old World mistletoe (*Viscum album*). Its berries were used to make birdlime.

7. For "oksel" which literally means the pit of one's arm. Still used in the Netherlands as a term in botany. Towards the end of the sixteenth century, the Dutch made the deliberate choice to eschew Latin

and Greek terminology in science, and preferred instead original vernacular compounds. This is one example. In modern "English" terminology the term would be "axil," but that was not standard usage until the end of the eighteenth century.

8. The iris.

9. The width of a finger was about 0.30 inch.

10. For the original "doortogen met," which is a rare usage of *doortiegen*. Since the Middle Ages this verb had been used only in the imperfect and the past participial forms. I think Rumphius has in mind the sense of something extending across something else, and not the notion of something woven through something else, which is also possible in Dutch.

11. For "geut," variant of *goot*, a channel to convey liquid away, such as a gutter on a house.

12. The satyr orchid is today restricted to the species *Coeloglossum bracteatum*, a terrestrial plant from the cooler regions. Rumphius uses "Satyrium" in a generic sense. Ancient authors, who knew the roots better than the living flower, ascribed erotic powers to this plant, basing their belief on the shape of the roots.

Orchis is the Greek word for testicle, and the plant was called this because the tuberous roots resemble male gonads. Pliny was also struck by those remarkable plants. In book 26, chapter 62, of his *Natural History*, he puts the *orchis* "high on the list of wonders." Because the "twin roots look similar to testicles" the plant is said to arouse sexual desire and was given the alternative name: *satyrion.* Yet another kind he calls *satyrios orchis* and says that it prefers to be near the sea. When mixed with sheep's milk, "orchis" will induce erections, but if taken with water it will have the opposite effect. See Pliny, *Natural History*, 7:336–339; hereafter referred to as Pliny, with volume and page number(s).

Pliny's text is not very clear, but the identification of the plant's properties with the physical feature of its roots—the doctrine of signatures—survived in the popular belief that orchids were an aphrodisiac, whence their other name which Rumphius also provides: *Satyria.*

13. Rumphius is trying to convey to his readers the decorative pat-

terns on the petals, which he compares here to Hebrew characters, probably Rashi script, for instance: שׁוֹמֵר

14. *Blimbing* or *belimbing* is the star fruit, *Averrhoa carambola* L., to be found throughout the archipelago. It is an apt comparison. Rumphius describes the blimbing tree in 1.30.1:115–118.

15. He is referring to the arches that rise from the circlet, from front to back, or side to side, in a continuing loop.

16. For the Dutch verb *verstuiven.* This exclusively West-Germanic word (*stäuben* in German) propagated the beautiful Dutch compound noun *stuifmeel,* for "pollen." A cognate, *stive,* was once current in Pembrokeshire, England, for "dust," specifically the floating dust of flour during the operation of grinding (*OED*).

17. This is an important passage, for it implies that Rumphius entertained the notion that orchids propagated by wind-born seed. Orchid seed was virtually unknown at the time.

18. "Manga" is the well-known mango tree (*Mangifera indica* L.) which Rumphius described at length in 1.21.1:93–97. Smith notes (M, p. 177) that Hasskarl suggested this plant might be *Cymbidium wallichii* Lindl. Smith is not certain about this.

19. A "hand" was considered the equivalent of four inches.

20. What Rumphius calls "Dart Root" in Dutch is *bakung* in Indonesian, *Crinum asiaticum* L., described by him in 11.45.6:155–159.

21. This refers most likely to what in Latin palaeography is called "Square Capitals" such as the following:

OPARENSE

See Thompson, *An Introduction to Greek and Latin Palaeography*, pp. 272–275.

22. Rumphius is presumably referring to an ancient Samaritan script, common to a part of Palestine in the fourth century B.C. See Crown, "Samaritan Minuscule Palaeography," *Bulletin*, pp. 330–368. There was a "square or majuscule" script "which is a developed form of the palaeo-Hebrew script" and a "minuscule or cursive, which is a flowing and undecorated script" (p. 330). It is probable that Rumphius has the majuscule script in mind, for that is the one he most likely saw since it was the official script used for religious works.

23. Smith (M, p. 177) states that what Rumphius baptized "Coconut Orchid" was referred to by Blume to *Arachnis flos aeris Rchb.f.* but is again (see n. 18) doubtful that this is correct. De Wit, however, begs to differ: ". . . but I submit that Rumphius was aware of the presence of *A. flos aëris* on Java, that it differed from *G. scriptum,* and that it can be deduced that this Bornean endemic was an ornamental in Java since the first half of the seventeenth century or earlier" (p. 62).

24. *Lida* is the Indonesian word for "tongue."

25. "Bonga" is *bunga* and means "flower," and *putri* can mean "princess," hence the "Princess Flower," which, according to Rumphius, is what the name on Ternate, *Saja baki* (*baké* or *boki*), also means, as well as the Latin "Flos principissae."

26. Also spelled "keringsing" and "garingsing." *Kain geringsing*—which means "cloth that does not make you fall ill," i.e., perhaps simply "health"—is an ancient type of weaving that most likely originated in western India. It is a sacred textile, woven in double ikat, primarily from Bali. The cloths were used to ward off evil influences, and were employed only in rituals. They are now exclusively woven in the village called Tenganan Paperinsingan (see illustration on page 109).

27. A misprint: no "r."

28. Most likely a misprint because "lacra" or "lacre" would have something to do with sealing wax or lacquer. Perhaps what was meant was the popular Portuguese word *lacrau* (Spanish: *alacran*), which meant "scorpion."

Ceremonial cloth, *geringsing wayang puteri*, from Bali.
Cotton, double-ikat, from beginning of the twentieth century.
27806 Collection Wereldmuseum Rotterdam.

29. Although *api* is the common Indonesian word for "fire," Rumphius has *pohon api-api* in mind, which is a name for mangrove trees.

30. There is some confusion here, it seems to me. Van Bemmel, in *Rumphius Memorial Volume*, p. 55 (hereafter *MV,* with page number[s]), says that this bird might be *Dicaeum vulneratum* (Wallace), but the name, "Cacopit" or "Kakopit," and Rumphius' descriptions here, in 5:61, and in 2:149, seem to fit *Nectarinia aspasia* better. This "Sunbird" of the family Nectariniidae is described as "Black Sunbird" in Beehler, Pratt, and Zimmerman, *Birds of New Guinea*, p. 192. They provide the illustration on page 110:

See plate 52 for an illustration from Rumphius' era.

31. Mangroves.

32. See 5:61.

33. The popular *kenari* tree, *Canarium commune* L.

♀   ♂

From Bruce M. Beehler, Thane K. Pratt, and Dale A. Zimmerman,
Birds of New Guinea. Copyright © by Princeton University Press.
Reprinted by permission of Princeton University Press.

34. This passage shows, according to De Wit (p. 63), that Rumphius understood that epiphytes are not parasites.

35. An example of the botanical experiments that Rumphius constantly performed in his small, private hortus botanicus in eastern Indonesia.

36. The second passage that corroborates the assertion in n. 34.

37. With "Waringin" trees, also known in English as banyan trees, Rumphius is referring specifically to what he called the "Small-leaved Waringin" or *Ficus benjamina* L., described in 5.5.3:139–142, esp. 140. This is the first correct mention of how this species propagates (De Wit, p. 63).

38. "Viscum" is what Rumphius calls "Ambonese Mistletoe" and De Wit (*MV*, p. 459) identifies as *Amylotheca triflora* (Span.) Danser. Described in 6.32.5:60–62, esp. p. 61.

39. Once better known as "Katjang," now spelled *kacang*, this is the peanut (*Arachis hypogaea* L.).

40. "Whitlow" was in the original the succinct compound noun *nagelzweer*. This refers to a festering sore or ulcer at the topmost finger joint, usually near the nail. This is also called *vijt* in Dutch, which might well be the first component ("whit") of the English noun.

41. "Curcuma" is *kunyit, Curcuma domestica* Val., a kind of yellow curry, indispensable in Indonesian cooking.

42. The Latinized form of Charles de l'Escluse (1526–1609), Belgian scholar born in Arras, in northern France. He was educated at the universities of Ghent, Louvain, and Wittenberg and studied medicine under the famous Rondelet at the University of Montpellier. He became a mentor of the son of Fugger, the wealthy banker. In 1564 he traveled to Spain and Portugal and came across Orta's work. In England in 1571 Clusius found the work in Spanish on medicinal plants from the New World by Nicolas Monardes, a Spanish physician from Seville, entitled (in Clusius' translation) *De simplicibus medicamentis ex occidentali India delatis quorum in medicina usus est*, and during another stay in England obtained a copy of the work by Cristóbal Acosta entitled *Tractado de las drogas, y medicinas de las Indias orientales*. Clusius became prefect of the Imperial Garden in Vienna and later the director of the botanical garden of the University in Leyden. He succeeded to the chair held by Dodoens at the latter's death.

What Clusius appears to have done is collect works on botany and natural history such as the Iberian trio just mentioned, abridge them, translate the abbreviated version into Latin, then annotate and correct them. In some cases—especially in that of Garcia da Orta—the original work was supplanted by this later version, so the problem arises that one will often find references to Carolus Clusius' work when in fact it was someone else's.

Clusius' first collaborative effort was on Rondelet's *De piscibus marinis libri XVIII*, and he also translated Dodoens' *Cruydeboeck* into French as *Histoire des plantes* (1557). Among his original works are a flora of Spain (1576) and one on Hungary and Austria (1583).

43. Carolus Clusius, *Rariorum plantarum historia* (Antwerp: Plantin, 1601). This volume contained descriptions and illustrations of European plants.

44. This refers to the Flemish botanist Rembert Dodoens (1518–1585). He studied in Louvain, in France, and in Italy, and although he became a physician, Dodonaeus was primarily interested in botany. He was in Vienna from 1574 to 1580; there he met Clusius and became the personal physician to the Emperor Maximilian II and his successor

Rudolph II. He was appointed a professor in Leyden in 1582, a position he held until his death, when his chair went to Clusius. He wrote
many scientific works, mostly published in Antwerp and printed by
Plantin. Primarily of interest in the present context are his herbals. In
1554 he published in Antwerp a herbal entitled *De stirpium historia*, which
was reprinted with additional material in two volumes in 1559. In 1554
a Dutch version had been published as *Cruydeboeck*, and reprinted in
1563. This same work appeared in a French translation by Charles de
l'Escluse (Clusius) as *Histoire des plantes* (1557), and in an English translation in 1578 (reprinted in 1586, 1595, 1600, 1619). His major work is *Stirpium
historiae pemptades sex sive libri XXX*, published by Plantin in Antwerp in
1583 and reprinted in 1616. This was published in a Dutch translation in
Leyden in 1608 as *Herborius, seu Cruydeboeck van Rembertus Dodonaeus*. The
famous *Herball* (1597) by John Gerard (1545–1612) was an adaptation of
Dodonaeus' *Stirpium historiae pemptades*. Since Gerard's text is fundamen-
tally the same as that of Dodonaeus' 1583 *Herbal*, one can consult it for
references to the work of the Flemish botanist. "Calceolus Mariae,"
or the Lady's Slipper, is described in Gerard's *Herbal* in bk. 2, ch. 112.
Gerard, p. 443.

45. One of those tireless compilers that belong to the earlier history of natural science, Conrad Gesner (1516–1565) had a difficult youth.
When Gesner was still a teenager, his father, a follower of Zwingli,
was killed, along with Zwingli, at the Battle of Kappel on October 11,
1531, and young Conrad was left without sufficient financial resources.
But he succeeded in his studies in Paris, and in Montpellier, where he
attended the lectures of Rondolet. The stamina of people like Gesner is amazing. He traveled a great deal, no sinecure in the sixteenth
century, practiced medicine (in fact, while administering to victims
of the plague in Basel, he succumbed to the disease himself), and
helped various colleagues. Yet before he was thirty he published his
huge *Biblioteca universalis*, a catalog of all past writers in Latin, Greek,
and Hebrew, and at the age of twenty-four he was appointed a professor of medicine, physics, and ethics in Switzerland. He was a scholar
of Greek, Latin, and Hebrew, a botanist, and the owner of a curi-

osity cabinet that contained items he had collected during his many travels. His very important botanical work was not well known for quite some time. In 1542 he published a *Catalogus Plantarum Latinae, Graecae, Germaniae et Galliae,* which was used for at least two centuries. In 1561 he published *De hortis Germanicae,* which contains five orchids. "Gesner collected plants for 20 years and made more than 1500 drawings, of which he published only a few during his life," notes Jacquet (p. 64). These drawings were not found until the early part of the twentieth century and not published until the last quarter. On the basis of drawings of several orchid species, Arditti concluded that Gesner was the first to *draw* orchid seeds, but Rumphius remains the first to *describe* them. For Gesner see Jacquet, pp. 63–64. For Gesner and orchid seed, see Wehner, Zierau, and Arditti, "Plinius Germanicus and Plinius Indicus."

46. *Κοσμο-σάνδαλον* is the Doric name of ὑάκινθος, the hyacinth. The ancient Greek name included several different flowers. "Kosmos" here does not mean "world" or "universe" but "ornament," "decoration," or "embellishment." Hence the expressive phrase for this flower means "Embellished Sandal." Lawler reports that experts have suggested this plant was the orchid *Ophrys ferrum-equinum* Desf. See Lawler, esp. p. 33. Others have suggested *Cypripedium calceolus* L.; see Jacquet, p. 39.

47. Pausanias flourished around 150 A.D. He was a Greek traveler and geographer who knew Italy, Rome, Greece, Egypt, and Palestine. He is especially remembered for his "Description of Greece." The plant was mentioned in the following context. During a chthonian festival at Demeter's sanctuary in Corinth, a procession was held that included children who wore wreaths. "Their wreaths are woven of the flower called by the natives cosmosandalon, which, from its size and colour, seems to me to be an iris; it even has inscribed upon it the same letters of mourning." Pausanias, *Description of Greece,* 1:440–443.

48. *Χιλιο-δύναμις* is the plant πολεμώνιον mentioned by Dioscorides, in his *Materia medica,* 4.8(9). The polemonion plant is described by Dioscorides as follows (illustration included):

Polemonion.

Polemonium coeruleum Polemonia, but some call it Philetaeria, ye Cappadocians call it Chiliodynamis. It has little thin branches, winged, but leaves a little greater than Rue, but longer aunswerable to those of Polygonum, or of Calaminth, but on ye top of them are as it were Corymbi, in which is a black seed. Ye root a cubit long, whitish, like to Struthium. It grows in hilly and rough places. The root of this is drank in wine against venemous beasts, & ye Dysentery, & ye Dysurie, and the Sciatica, with water. It is given to ye splenicall, as much as a dragm, with Acetum. And ye roote of this is hanged about one against ye stroke of a Scorpion. And they say that they which have this shall not be beaten & though they be smitten, yet they shall suffer nothing; & being chewed it easeth also ye toothache. (Quoted from: *The Greek Herbal of Dioscorides*, pp. 406–407.)

This is not an orchid but a species, *Polemonium coeruleum*, of the genus *Polemonium*, Polemoniaceae family, also known as Greek Valerian. It is native to temperate climes.

49. This means "Tiger Flower." One of the vernacular names for the orchid under discussion was "Tiger Orchid."

50. See Gerard, p. 122.

51. "Hieronymus Tragus" is the Latinized form of the name of the German botanist Jeremy Bock (1498–1554). His herbal, *Neu Kreütter Büch*, was published in 1538 and was not illustrated. Illustrated editions appeared in 1546 and 1552. The 1546 edition mentions eighteen orchids. Rumphius might be referring to the following edition: Hieronymi Tragi, *De stirpium, maxime earum, in Germania* (Strasbourg: V. Rihelius, 1552).

52. Athanasius Kircher (1601–1680) was not a botanist. A German scholar who became a Jesuit in 1618, he assumed the post of professor in Würzburg until the Thirty Years War forced him to flee to Avignon in France. The pope summoned him to Rome, where Kircher taught mathematics at the Collegium Romanum, and, later, studied hieroglyphs and archaeology. He was the first scholar to draw attention to hieroglyphs. He wrote a large number of books, among which one on China— *China illustrata* (published in Amsterdam in 1667)—and one on Egyptian hieroglyphs—*Oedipus aegyptiacus* (4 vols., published in Rome between 1652 and 1654)—are perhaps the most significant. Kircher had a great interest in Oriental languages, and when he was teaching in Rome, he interviewed many of the missionaries returning from China. His compilation of information on China became famous and very influential. A Dutch translation appeared in 1668, a French one in 1670, and a (partial) English translation in 1669.

The book Rumphius is referring to, *Mundus subterraneus* (published in 2 vols. in Amsterdam in 1664–1665), was a very strange text about what one might call telluric sciences, aspects of the earth. Rumphius must have owned a copy and knew it well. He also quotes from it in his *Ambonese Curiosity Cabinet.*

53. Kircher's strange tale echoes the then prevalent theory of spontaneous generation (abiogenesis) for these plants. Propagation by means of seed was still unknown. Kirchner's notions were based on the then prevalent belief that insects, such as bees or wasps, generated

from dead bulls and horses, a notion derived from Virgil and the Old Testament. I also think Kircher and others were specifically thinking of the genus *Ophrys*, which includes plants that are small and like to grow in places such as meadows and heath, i.e., places where cattle roam. Furthermore, species of *Ophrys* are remarkable for their mimicry of insects. The lips of various *Ophrys* species look very much like bees, wasps, or flies. The plant mimics because it lacks nectar and needs to entice insects to come and inadvertently remove pollen, which they then transmit to a neighboring orchid that also looks like an enticing insect. From the passage preceding these quotes, one can deduce, without hesitation, that Rumphius had his doubts about such peculiar notions of provenance, and inclined to his own (correct) intuition about orchid seed.

54. "Coagulum terrae" is mentioned by Pliny in 27.44.7:430–431. The translator, W. H. S. Jones, considers this plant "earth rennet" while the index (p. 501 of vol. 7) glosses it as "probably bedstraw [or] *Galium verum*." The botanist Kreutzer assumes this same plant to be *Neottia nidus avis* (L.) Rich. See Jacquet, p. 43.

55. Dr. Henk van der Werff came to my rescue here. Gesner mentioned "Orobanche" in *Historia plantarum et vires ex Dioscoride*, p. 185.

Theophrastus first mentioned "orobanche" in his *Enquiry into Plants*, bk. 8, ch. 8; see *Enquiry into Plants*, Loeb ed., 2:194–195. Theophrastus' "orobanche" seems to have been a plant called "dodder" in English (*Cuscuta europea*). Dioscorides (bk. II, no. 172) had most likely the modern botanical notion of broom-rape (a root parasite) in mind. Pliny (bk. 18, Latin paragraph 155, and bk. 22, Latin paragraph 80) used the name both ways; the first mention is orobanche as dodder, the second as broom-rape. Properly, orobanche is the latter, a root parasite.

How could Rumphius consider Orobanche related to an orchid? Van der Werff provides the following comment. Orobanche, the root parasite, "is not unlike some terrestrial orchids. Terrestrial orchids can be saprophytic (i.e. they are parasitic on fungi), lack chlorophyll completely, and are also leafless. Orobanche also has rather elaborate flowers and I can certainly see a superficial resemblance between Orobanche and some terrestrial orchids. Of course, from a point of view of plant classification, Orobanche is very far removed from orchids" (written communication).

56. Jean Bauhin (1541–1612) came from a Parisian medical family that converted to Protestantism and fled to Switzerland. Bauhin studied in Basel and became a protégé of Gesner's in 1560. He also studied in Montpellier under Rondolet and obtained his medical degree in 1562. Between 1563 and 1567 he had a medical practice in Lyons, where he survived the 1564 plague epidemic. In 1572 he settled down for the rest of his life in Montbéliard in the French Jura at the court of the Duke of Würtenberg. Bauhin established several botanic gardens. His main work, presumably the one Rumphius is referring to, was *Historia Plantarum Universalis*, which he started working on in 1570 and left unfinished at his death. It was not published until 1650.

57. Today *Viscum* is a genus of semi-parasitic plants like mistletoe.

58. "Struik" in the original, which normally means "shrub," but which once (though the usage is now obsolete) could refer to the trunk of a tree (*WNT*).

59. Most chapters in Rumphius' *Herbal* ends with a "Comment" — "Aanmerking" in Dutch and "Observatio" in Latin. They were written by Johannes Burman (1707–1778), a professor of botany and director of the Municipal Botanical Garden in Amsterdam. Burman translated Rumphius' *Herbal* into Latin, and was responsible for getting it published (with great difficulty) between 1741 and 1755, in an edition that printed his Latin translation in columns of text parallel to the Dutch original. I would surmise that his comments were first written in Latin and then translated into Dutch. They are little more than botanical notes on taxonomy, hence often cryptic. He was the first to compare the flora of Ceylon (Sri Lanka), which he had indexed alphabetically in 1737 in his *Thesaurus Zeylanicus*, with that of the *Hortus Malabaricus* by Van Reede tot Drakenstein. (See next note.)

60. This is a reference to the *Hortus Malabaricus*, the only work of tropical botany to rival Rumphius', which was published in twelve volumes in Amsterdam between 1678 and 1693. Its author, who was really

a facilitator more than anything else, was Hendrik Adriaan van Reede tot Drakenstein (1636–1691). Of Dutch nobility, Van Reede became a high official in the service of the Dutch East Indies Company, better known by its acronym VOC (Verenigde Oost-Indische Compagnie). Most of his official career was spent in India (the Malabar coast) and Ceylon. He lived extravagantly, yet his superiors chose him in 1684 to act as a kind of inspector-general to root out corruption in the Company's ranks. He died on board ship on the way from Ceylon to India and was rumored to have been poisoned by his enemies. He was buried with great pomp in Surat.

For his magnum opus, Van Reede used something of a college of local Malabar Brahmin experts, and solicited the support of Malabar nobility. The botanical information they supplied was reviewed and indexed by European experts, such as the Carmelite Monk Matthew of St. Joseph, Paul Hermann, a professor of botany, the physician (and hence, by necessity, botanist) Willem ten Rhijne in Batavia (the VOC's capital on Java), and others, and the manuscript conveyed to the Netherlands. There it was reviewed once again and augmented with botanical information by yet another tier of experts, such as Jan Commelin. Because of his political clout and connections, Van Reede saw most of his text published during his lifetime, something that Rumphius was never able to enjoy. The best study, and in English, on Van Reede and his *Hortus Malabaricus* is by J. Heniger, hereafter referred to as Heniger, with page number(s). Future references to the Malabar herbal will be to *Hortus Malabaricus*, with the volume and page number(s). Rumphius knew the first ten volumes and "compared more than 150 plants with Van Reede's plants" (Heniger, p. 174). Orchids are listed in the last (twelfth) volume of the *Hortus Malabaricus*, but Rumphius never saw volumes 11 and 12.

The reference to "Ansjeli Maravara," the plant's Malayalam name, is *Hortus Malabaricus*, 12:1–4 (first illustration), which Linnaeus (1753) listed as a species of the genus *Epidendrum*.

61. Jan Commelin (1629–1692) was the second commentator of the *Hortus Malabaricus*, and the editor of volumes 2 through 12. His notes

were printed in the text. His nephew, Caspar Commelin (1667–1731), became a renowned botanist, but Jan Commelin himself was not a professional botanist, though, like many of his compatriots at the time, he became a passionate and quite competent amateur. He made a career in the lucrative apothecary business and gradually rose in Amsterdam's municipal hierarchy. He published several catalogi on Dutch flora and in 1682 was appointed managing director of the newly established medical botanical garden in Amsterdam. It soon rivaled its predecessor in Leiden. See Heniger, pp. 160–161.

62. This was a literal translation of Commelin's Latin inscription in the twelfth volume of the *Hortus Malabaricus:* "Orchis Abortiva Aizoides Malanariensis, flore odoratissimo variegato, intus aviculam repraesentante."

63. I presume this refers to Caspar Commelin, *Flora Malabarica sive Horti Malabarici Catalogus Exhibens Omnium ejusdem Plantarum nomina* (Leiden, 1696).

64. Sir Hans Sloane (1660–1753), a physician and naturalist, accompanied Monck to Jamaica from 1687 to 1698, and became Queen Anne's physician in 1712. He was president of the Royal Society from 1727 to 1740, and his library and herbarium provided the foundation for the British Museum. The abbreviation refers to Sloane's *Catalogus plantarum quae in insula Jamaica sponte proveniunt* (London: D. Brown, 1696).

65. Hans Sloane, *A voyage to the Islands Madera, Barbados, Nieves, S. Christophers and Jamaica,* 2 vols. (London: printed for the author, 1707–1725).

Chapter Two

1. Original text in 11.2.6:99–100.

Phalaenopsis amabilis (L.) Blume. Smith proceeds to note that the other two forms of this monopodial orchid as distinguished by Rumphius "are referable to the same species. It is well known that the flowers of *Phalaenopsis amabilis* (L.) Blume vary considerably in size, in the form of the sepals, petals, lip, and especially in the size and markings of the yellow area on the lip. Specimens with the sepal purplish on the outside are not rare." De Wit, however, begs to differ; see nn. 6 and 7. This orchid was chosen as Indonesia's national flower; see Comber, p. 306.

2. This text contains some tricky translation problems. The original here was "chordelen," which I presume to be a variant of *gordelen*, to encompass with a belt or ceinture.

3. For "verward," which normally means "confused," but this is botany.

4. For "wild."

5. For "met donker-bruine linien gespikkelt." There is a contradiction here. *Gespikkelt* can only mean "speckled," "dotted," "spotted," and the like. Globular markings cannot correspond to lines (*linien*), so I dropped the main Dutch verb in my rendition.

6. Smith states this is the same species but De Wit (p. 66) wonders if it might be related to *Phalaenopsis deliciosa* Rchb. f. (*Phalaenopsis hebe* Rchb.f.).

7. De Wit again demurs and wonders if this might be *Dendrobium crumenatum* Swartz (p. 66). I should add here that De Wit's text reads as if he considered Rumphius' passage starting with "Name" as referring to this contested species. But its real antecedent is *Phalaenopsis amabilis*.

8. This means "the Great White Orchid." The first Malay phrase mans the same thing.

9. "Bombo" is a misprint for "Pombo," a local word for "dove." *Terbang* is standard Indonesian for "flying," hence "Flying Dove," a name adopted in Dutch.

10. Luhu was a region on Hoamoal or "Little Ceram."

11. "Kinar" was the Ambonese name for the tree *Kleinhovia hospita* L. described by Rumphius in 5.27.3:177–178.

12. Mango tree.

13. "Zeel" in the original, which has a large number of very specific meanings, of which rope is the most generic and which recalls the phrase "forest rope" that Rumphius uses for the (at the time unknown noun) *liana*.

14. "Small White Angrec" is *Dendrobium ephemerum* J. J. Sm. (M, p. 174).

15. For "gefronst."

16. "Riddersporen" in the original. Delphiniums.

17. For "ingelaten," a difficult usage here.

18. For "luchtig." Strange usage. The primary and most common meaning of *luchtig* is "airy," which has little significance here; the second most common meaning is "cheerful," which is also inappropriate. I think what Rumphius meant was either a hill without dense tree coverage, or "cool," the latter a specific meaning during his century especially common among sailors: i.e., a cool breeze (*een luchtig windje*). I opted for the former.

19. *Melaleuca leucadendron* L. trees that produce the once profitable medicinal oil.

20. For "bygewas." "Parasitic" was not commonly used until the eighteenth century.

21. "Tufts of hair" for "lokken."

22. This tropical fern is most likely the plant reduced by Merrill to *Drynaria sparsisora* (Desv.) Moore (M, p. 68), and described by Rumphius in 10.55.6:78–81.

23. Indonesian for "Small White Orchid."

24. This does indeed mean "poor anggrek," but in the sense of pity or compassion. It is an expression heard countless times by anyone who has lived in the Indies. An equivalent is the Spanish *pobrecito.* However, I do not quite know what Rumphius has in mind here. See next note.

25. "Cassian," now *kasian,* is invoked by the Dutch word "slecht," which is intended to describe the plant's shape. Now *slecht* commonly has a clear pejorative meaning, but I do not think that this is what Rumphius meant to convey. Originally the word meant no more than "simple," "normal" (the old sense of "ordinary"), "orderly," "guileless." This is what Rumphius may have intended, thinking of comparing this flower with the more extravagant beauty of its fellow orchids.

26. De Wit (p. 68) suggests this might be *Dendrobium suaveolens* Schltr. and might be "closely allied to *Dend. ephemerum,* but there is no certainty."

27. "Daun subat" is, according to De Wit (p. 68), a *Dendrobium* sp., "probably *Dendrobium acinaciforme* Roxb." See ch. 9.

28. This is spelled "Ponnampou-marvara" in *Hortus Malabaricus*, 12: 708, third illustration.

Chapter Three

1. Original text in 11.3.6:101.

Smith (M, p. 179) lists this as *Renanthera moluccana* Bl.

2. "Zeeliger" in the original, hence the comparative of *zeel*, for which see n. 13 of the previous chapter. "Roping" was a noun used in Rumphius' century for "a ropy or rope-like formation" (*OED*).

3. For the original "in 't kreupel bos tussen de ruigte."

4. A span was the equivalent of about nine inches, hence the stem is about twenty-two inches long.

5. "The Red Orchid"; the Indonesian phrase means the same thing. De Wit (p. 68), though not disagreeing with J. J. Smith, thinks that this epiphyte could also be *Renanthera coccinea* Lour.

6. Now spelled *acar*, this refers to pickles or anything preserved in an acid liquid.

7. From the Latin, originally Greek, *capparis*, here a kind of tropical capers. Rumphius writes that the fruits of a small tree (*Carissa carandas* L.) were eaten either raw or, most often, after having been pickled. He describes it in the "Auctuarium" or 7. 74.7:57–58.

8. This plant has not been identified.

9. See ch. 6.

Chapter Four

1. Original text in 11.4.6:102.

Smith (M, p. 178) lists this orchid as *Vandopsis lissochiloides* (Gaudich.) Pfitz.

2. The Latin means: "The Fifth Orchid or the Small Inscribed Orchid."

3. Merrill (M, p. 383) classifies this mangrove tree as *Sonneratia caseolaris* (L.) Engl., which is described by Rumphius in 4.62.3:111–115.

4. "Waccat" was the Ambonese name for the tree just mentioned, also spelled *Wahat merah* or *Wakat merah.*

5. Now *rendah*, this Indonesian word means "humble" or "submissive."

6. See n. 25 of ch. 2.

7. De Wit (p. 69) gives the following identification for this tree: *Pisonia grandis* R. Br. var. *sylvestris* (T. et B.) Heim, while Merrill (M, p. 216) gives *Pisonia grandis* R.Br.

8. "Gomuto," also spelled "gemutu" or "gumuto," is the fiber, resembling horsehair, of the sugar palm *Areca pinnata* (Wurmb.) Merr.— a synonym for the more familiar name *Arenga saccharifera*—once used to make rope or thatch.

Chapter Five

1. Original text in 11.5.6:102–104.
"The Sixth Orchid, the Musk or Odoriferous Orchid." Comber identifies this as *Dendrobium bicaudatum* Reinw. ex Lindl. De Wit (p. 70), however, opts for *Dendrobium strebloceras* Rchb.f.; Mr. Comber informed me that the latter is only known on Halmahera.

2. "Houseleek" is *huislook* in modern Dutch, but Rumphius had the more expressive older name for this succulent of the genus *Sempervivum:* "Donderbaart," which means "Thunderbeard." Indeed, the plant was once also known as "Barba Iovis" (*Sempervivum tectorum* L.).

3. "Spadulen" in the original. The "d" is in the Latin as well, but I am assuming this is a misprint for "spatulen" or spatulas. "Spatule," which entered English from Middle Dutch, was a common form in English in Rumphius' time, regularly used by such writers as Holland (translator of Pliny), Evelyn, and Sir Thomas Browne. By the way, with "Surgeons" we are talking of "Barber Surgeons," not our modern medical mechanics.

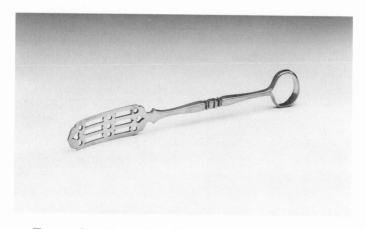

Tongspatel inv. Nr. 569. Copyright Museum Boerhaave in Leiden.
Photograph by Tom Haartsen.

4. "Cananga" is the favorite *kenanga* flower of the *Canangium odoratum* tree, described by Rumphius in 3.19.2:195–197.

5. The flowers of the "Tanjong" (now *tanjung*) tree, *Mimusops elengi* L., which, as Rumphius asserts, were considered "the Princess of tree-Flowers" in his day. He described it in 3.17.2:189–192.

6. De Wit (p. 70) thinks this orchid might be *Dendrobium moschatum* Swartz.

7. Rumphius meant Siva. The Balinese are Hindus, more specifically Sivaists. The Hindu god, whose name means "auspicious," has 1,008 epithets. Rumphius' "Dewa" is the Vedic word for a celestial power or supreme being, *deva.*

8. That is to say "musk."

9. Professor Arditti informed me in writing that this is most likely another "first," explaining it as follows: "In most orchids the sepals, petals and gynostemium (column) wither, die, and disappear. But in a few these parts turn green and persist. There are also cases, as described here by Rumphius, in which these parts may die but they still persist."

10. "Casturi" is *kasturi* or *kesturi* in Indonesian, that is to say civet, obtained from either ambergris, the civet cat, or the musk shrew.

11. See ch. 1.

12. See n. 2 of ch. 1.

13. See nn. 3 and 4 of ch. 4.

14. The "Seventh Orchid" is *Dendrobium bicaudatum* Reinw. ex Lindl. Smith contends that he does not see a significant difference between the plant depicted on plate 45 and the second figure on plate 46 (M, p. 174).

15. An ell is about twenty-seven and a half inches.

16. "Horsel" in the original. Spelled *horzel* in modern Dutch, of the family Tabanidae.

17. See n. 4.

18. The well-known champaca flower, *Michelia champaca* L., described by Rumphius in 3.21.2:199–201.

19. This is another interesting observation because, as J. Arditti pointed out to me in writing, "orchid flowers exhibit many interesting pest pollination phenomena [and the] closing of flowers is one of them. . . . Color changes are also common pest pollination phenomena. This is clearly another 'first' for Rumphius."

20. The "Seventh Orchid."

21. The "Champaca Orchid."

22. Mangroves.

Chapter Six

1. Original text in 11.6.6:104–105.
The "Eighth or Dusky Orchid" (M, p. 178) is *Vanda furva* (L.).

2. See ch. 2: the "Small White Orchid" or *Dendrobium ephemerum.*

3. See ch. 3: *Renanthera moluccana.*

4. The phrase means: "Small dark Orchid." "Glap" should be *gelap*, for "dark," "somber," "black." The chilling phrase *mata gelap*, or mental derangement, literally means "darkening of the eye" as if a black cloud of madness obscured sensible vision.

5. See ch. 2.

6. This sympodial epiphyte is now *Dendrobium bicaudatum* Reinw. ex Lindl., as J. B. Comber informed me.

7. A large genus of fleshy plants of the Crassulaceae family; he was probably referring to the houseleek again.

8. See ch. 5.

9. *Mimusops elengi* L. See n. 5 of ch. 5.

10. According to De Wit (p. 68), this might be *Dendrobium acinaciforme.*

11. "Capaha" was the name of a steep mountain near Hitu's northern coast, east of the Ela River. It was a seemingly impregnable stronghold for the Islamic forces of Tulukabessi, who were fighting the VOC. See Rumphius, *Ambonsche Landbeschrijving*, pp. 31–32.

12. "The Small Lemon Orchid."

13. The "Tenth or Narrow-Leaved Orchid" is (M, p. 178) *Luisia confusa* Rchb. f.

14. *Canarium* species.

15. Perhaps *Vigna sinensis* (L.) Hassk., described by Rumphius in 9.22.5:375–376 (see figure on page 127).

16. For "weiniger."

17. Bontius, "Historiae Naturalis & Medicae Liber Sextus. De Plantis, & Aromatibus," pp. 124–125. Bontius' plant is most likely a *Vanilla* species, as Henk van der Werff informed me.

18. What we know as "preserve" or "preserves."

Chapter Seven

1. Original text in 11.7.6:105.
For "geil." The dog odor that Rumphius smelled has been likened by others to the smell of goats. The flowers of the *Satyrium* orchid

$\frac{1}{2}$

Vigna sinensis, (L.). Savi, ex Hassk.
From J. J. Ochse, Tropische Groenten.

do indeed contain caproic acid, which has an unpleasant smell of goats. See Arditti, "Caproic Acid," *American Orchid Society Bulletin*, pp. 298–300.

2. The "Eleventh or Dog Orchid" is, according to Smith (M, p. 175), *Dendrobium anosmum* Lindl.

3. Now spelled *anjing*, the phrase means the same as the Latin: "Dog Orchid." One should remember that dogs were never favorites in Asia and, generally speaking, have a negative connotation.

4. *Kleinhovia hospita* L.; see n. 11 of ch. 2.

5. The only "pursed Angrek" in the next, interpolated chapter, is no. IV, which Rumphius called, in Latin, "Angraecum angustis cru-menis" or "Narrow-pursed Orchid" and which Smith identified as *Eria moluccana*. Smith states (M, p. 173) that the illustration does *not* depict *Eria moluccana*, but that the second figure on plate 47 is *Dendrobium papilio-niferum* J. J. Sm.

The Fifty Seventh Chapter of the Auctuarium

1. Original text in 11.6:106–109. The title tells us that this represents ch. 57 of the "Auctuarium" or "Addition" to the *Herbal* (for convenience' sake known as volume 7). This was written after the first six volumes were finished and was added without worrying about textual integration. The present text was originally intended for the "Auctuarium" but was lifted and placed here, leaving the following statement to represent ch. 57 in volume 7: "Some new species of *Angrek,* which were described and depicted before in Book eleven, Ch.7, vol. 6."

2. "Angraecum nervosum" is not a nervous plant; this means the "Sinewy Orchid" and was listed by Smith (M, p. 169) as *Coelogyne rumphii* Lindl. De Wit (p. 74) also suggests *Coelogyne celebensis* J. J. Sm. for this species.

3. "Kinar" was the Ambonese name for a common tree, which Rumphius also called "cattimarus." It is classified as *Kleinhovia hospita* L. and was described by Rumphius in 5.28.3:177–178. He knew this tree well because he had tried the sap of its leaves as a remedy for his deteriorating eyesight. "And the Native Masters dripped the sap of the selfsame leaves into my eyes, when my sight began to give way, in order to cleanse the eyes, and I did not feel anything at first, but shortly thereafter I felt a piercing sharpness that shot up into my brain, and it did not help me, perhaps because the disease was too pertinacious" (3:178).

4. Once popularly known as "Moluccan Ironwood," this tree is listed by Merrill (M, p. 255) as *Intsia bijuga* (Colebr.) Kuntze. Rumphius described it in 4.7.3:21–24.

5. See n. 2 of ch. 1.

6. See n. 16 of ch. 5.

7. The description of plate 48 was written by Burman, not Rumphius.

8. Plukenet, *Almagesti Botanici Mantissa.*

9. This refers to a Mexican orchid and a work on the natural history of Mexico. The Aztecs and the Maya were quite familiar with

orchids and cultivated the vanilla orchid in pre-Columbian times. The Aztec elite, especially Emperor Montezuma, flavored their chocolate with the fruits of the orchid which they called *tlilxochitl*, meaning "black flower," which most likely was *Vanilla planifolia*. *Xóchitl* is the word for "flower" in Nahuatl. The vanilla orchid was probably the first tropical orchid to become known in Europe. The Spaniards brought vanilla (and the tale of its provenance) to Europe in 1510, and Clusius published the first European botanical description of it in his *Exoticorum libri decem*, printed in 1605. Another scholar from the Netherlands (encountered in these pages and peripherally associated with Rumphius) who is part of the history of the vanilla orchid is Willem Piso (1611–1678), the Leiden doctor who published Bontius' texts. He was the first to use and print the word "vaynilla" in his seminal work on the natural history of Brazil, *De Indiae utriusque*, published in 1658 (see Lawler, p. 54). Present usage of the noun "vanilla" derives from Piso. One can tell from these rare reports of tropical orchids and from the dates when these occurred how, once again, incredibly early and comprehensive Rumphius was.

The Mexican orchid mentioned by Burman, "Chichultic Tepetlauxochite," is most likely a misprint for "Chichiltic tepetlauhxochitl" as Hernandez had it. I would venture the guess that the first half of the second word is the Nahuatl *tepétlatl*, which means "hard ground" and suggests that this orchid was a lithophyte, perhaps *Laelia speciosa* (which is how Berliocchi, *The Orchid in Lore and Legend*, identifies it in the caption on p. 40; for Berliocchi's book see n. 7 of "The Petola Leaf," below). The work in which this particular orchid was pictured was executed by Francisco Hernández (1517–1587) and printed in a collaborative effort by several authors, with Recchi as the customary main author: Nardo Antonio Recchi, *Rerum medicarum Nouae Hispaniae thesaurus, seu, Plantarum animalium mineralium mexicanorum historia* (Rome: Vitalis Mascardi, 1651).

10. Comber identifies this as *Cleisostoma subulatum* Bl.

11. A low beach tree, *Excoecaria agallocha* L., that contains a blinding sap. Rumphius described it in 3.36.2:237–240.

12. ". . . beginnende Moer-nagel" in the original, where the first

word literally means "beginning." I assume he meant budding. The four different stages of the clove flower are shown here.

13. De Wit (p. 76) states that J. J. Smith, in an article published in 1926, classified this lithophytic orchid as *Vanda saxatilis* J. J. Sm. In Merrill's index from 1917, Smith merely said that it was a species of *Vanda* (M, p. 178), while in his earlier study of Ambonese orchids (1905), he had classified it as *Vanda crassiloba* (*Orchideen*, pp. 99–102).

14. *Hortus Malabaricus*, vol. 12, p. 11, figure 5: "Tsjerou-mau-maravara." Again, these comments were written by Burman, not Rumphius.

15. Plukenet, *Almagestum Botanicum*.

16. This is a literal translation of what Plukenet added in his commentary on the *Hortus Malabaricus*.

17. Plukenet, *Phytographia*.

18. Hermann, *Paradisus Batavus*.

19. This "Narrow-Purse Orchid" is *Eria moluccana* Schltr. & J. J. Sm.

20. Smith judges this plant to be "unrecognizable" (M, p. 179). De Wit conjectures a fern, either *Drymoglossum piloselloides* (L.) Presl. or *Cyclophorus nummarifolius* (Sw.) C. Chr. (p. 76).

21. See n. 2 of ch. 5.

22. This vine is most likely *Hoya rumphii* Blume, as Merrill asserts (M, p. 438). Rumphius described it in 9.77.5:470–471.

23. Smith offers only *Bulbophyllum* sp. for Rumphius' "Single-Flower Angrek," but adds: "The description of this plant in almost every point applies to *Bulbophyllum grandiflorum* Blume, but so far as I know Blume's species has not been recorded from Amboina" (M, p. 177). De Wit (p. 78) adds the possibility: *Bulbophyllum uniflorum* (Bl.) Hassk.

24. See ch. 7.

25. Smith (M, p. 172) reduced this to *Liparis treubii* J. J. Sm. De Wit (p. 78) thought that it might be *Liparis condylobulbon* Rchb. f. His reason was that "the genus *Liparis* in the Moluccas and Indonesia is very much in need of revision."

26. The "Gajang tree," more often "gajam" or "gajanus," is a tall tree, *Inocarpu sedulis* Forst. (M, p. 273). Rumphius described it in 1.55.1:170–171.

27. Rumphius really called it the "Indies Lily," and "Casi selan" he spelled in the chapter describing it—11.47.6:161–162—"casse selan," otherwise written "kasèsèlan," which is presumably Balinese. This plant is *Pancratium zeylanicum* L.

28. "Kattensteert" in the original. Burman takes this literally to be a cat's tail ("ut totus caulis caudam felis referat longam"), but I think Rumphius had the botanical meaning in mind. However, *katten-steert* refers to so many different plants that I will not hazard a guess as to which one he had in mind.

29. Rumphius might be talking about a valley near a river on Hoamoal, Seram's western peninsula, otherwise known as "Little Ceram," about two or three miles above Luhu.

30. For the very rare usage of *slensen;* the *WNT* quotes Rumphius to illustrate the verb's usage.

31. Smith (M, p. 176) offers only *Dendrobium* sp.

32. *Eugenia* sp.

33. Smith (M, p. 179) says only that "the plant described by Rumphius evidently belongs in the *Sarcanthinae.*" De Wit has nothing to add. *Taenia* (which Latin took over directly from Greek) originally meant a hairband, a ribbon—by extension a kind of fish, a tape worm, even a reef.

34. Rumphius uses the diminutive *riempje,* which I translate as "thong," in the older sense of a very thin strip of leather, used as a lace or strap.

35. This "Woolly [or Downy] Orchid" is a species of *Eria* (M, p. 177) according to Smith. De Wit offers: *Eria monostachya* Lindl. (p. 81).

36. I am sure Rumphius had a heraldic lion in mind: rampant, with a long, curved tongue sticking out of its open (i.e., "roaring") mouth. Such rampant lions were common armorial bearings in the Low Countries.

37. Perhaps a strange spelling of Tulehu, a town on Hitu's eastern coast, across from Haruku Island.

Chapter Eight

1. Original text in 11.8.6:109-110.

Smith (M, pp. 175-176) says only that this is a species of *Dendrobium*. De Wit (p. 81) offers no alternatives.

2. *Eugenia* sp.

3. A reddish pigment obtained from a layer around the seeds of (what is now) a common tall shrub, *Bixa orellana* L. Rumphius called it the "Paint Tree," also "Galuga," and "Pigmentaria" in 2.28.2:79-81.

4. This means the "Purple or Bare Orchid."

5. The "Jambu Orchid."

6. The "Cassomba Orchid."

7. Smith (M, p. 175) has no doubt this is *Dendrobium purpureum* Roxb.

8. This second species Rumphius called the "Purple Forest Orchid."

9. What we call the banyan tree, *Ficus benjamina* L., described by Rumphius in 5.5.3:139–142.

10. Perhaps the cemara tree, *Casuarina equisetifolia* L.

11. The clove tree, *Syzygium aromaticum* (L.) Merr. & Perry, is described at length by Rumphius in 2.1–4.2:1–13.

12. Literally "fish eye," it can also refer to a wart or pockmark. For "whitlow" see n. 40 of ch. 1.

13. See ch. 9.

14. *Hortus Malabaricus*, vol. 12, p. 9, fig. 4.

Chapter Nine

1. Original text in 11.9.6:110–112.
This sense of a "toady" existed in Rumphius' day, but not the botanical connotation of a parasite living off the nutriment of another plant. The latter usage was not recorded until after his death, during the first quarter of the eighteenth century.

2. Smith (M, p. 175) identified this orchid as *Dendrobium moluccense* J. J. Sm. Rumphius' Latin phrase means: "Small Suppliant Plant."

3. This was spelled "geel" in the original text, a word that means "yellow" in Dutch, but which I construe to be a misprint for "heel."

4. A wonderful phrase in the original: "lange in haar wezen blyvende." Arditti comments that this "is clearly a succulent orchid [and] longevity of succulent leaves is a known characteristic at present" (personal communication).

5. "Mai bloempjes" in the original. An old word for *Convallaria majalis*. No longer in use.

6. De Wit (p. 82) states that this is more likely a deep red.

7. "Subat" as a verb was colonial usage for "to coax" or "wheedle," in the sense of "butter up." Derived from *sobat* (friend) and spelled *soebatten*, it became part of continental Dutch, but it is not proper Indonesian.

8. In 10.7.6:12, where he called it "Gramen supplex" (a phrase he uses below) and "rompot or daun subat." De Wit (*MV,* p. 435) lists it as *Digitaria adscendens* (H.B.K.) Henr.

9. Smith (M, p. 173) labels the "First Large Suppliant Plant" *Dendrobium acinaciforme* Roxb.

10. "Parampuan" is properly *perempuan,* the word for "woman."

11. "Yver" in the original, which today commonly means effort, diligence, perhaps "ardor" in a figurative sense. But in Rumphius' day it could well mean "lust," "desire," a "passionate love." The word itself derives from the German *eifer,* a substantive that did not become current in Germany until Luther's vernacular translation of the Bible. It entered Dutch along with the vernacular Bible.

12. Elsewhere Rumphius calls this "Hieroglyphic Grammar" a "Grammatica Symbolica." What he has in mind is a language of flowers, whereby each particular plant represents an emotion or desire, a common knowledge shared by the native populace. A code based on nature's flora, it is a perfect example of semiotics since such a language of flowers is a system "that enable[s] human beings to perceive certain events or entities as signs, bearing meaning": Scholes, *Semiotics,* p. ix.

A note of caution: I am *not* speaking of emblematic or religious moralizing, which is how most scholars will discuss, for instance, Dutch flower painting. See Tyler, *Dutch Flower Painting 1600–1720,* esp. pp. 43–76. Even though Rumphius was a practicing Protestant, he was not a simple morals monger. He rather liked this floral stenography, a shorthand for illiterate people who needed to convey their desires without calling attention to their enterprise. In the text on the grass "Gramen supplex," mentioned in n. 8, he praises the economy of this semiotic code. He states that this grass had no particular use except that the Malay and Ternatan women include it in their "Grammar" (*Letterkunst*) since "if they want to write a Request to someone, wherewith they want to beg for forgiveness for some faults, something we have to do with many letters and Compliments, they accomplish this quite simply by sending a single twig of this grass, since its folded and flattened leaflets, represent the folded hands of whoever is begging for forgiveness" (6:12).

Such a floral code was once also used in Europe, and in the United States, particularly in the nineteenth century. It was particularly useful to lovers. See Osgood, *The Poetry of Flowers.* On p. 23 Osgood states the usage of flowers in this manner as follows: they were "ingeniously made emblematical of our most delicate sentiments; they do, in fact, utter in 'silent eloquence' a language better than writing"; in this way flowers make it "possible to quarrel, reproach, or send letters of passion, friendship, or civility, or even of news, without ever inking the fingers" (p. 22).

13. I think he is referring to "mamacurs" or "makurs," glass armlets held in great esteem by the Ceramese Alfurs. See *ACC,* pp. 276–278.

14. Perhaps a *Dendrobium* sp. but Smith judges the description to be "so vague that it is not even certain that the plant described by Rumphius belongs in the genus *Dendrobium*" (M, p. 176). De Wit (p. 84) is "even doubtful that an orchid was described." In any case, no illustration is given.

15. See n. 8.

16. In the original: "zy staan ook in malkander geschikt" — a troublesome phrase. I take *schikken* here to be a synonym for *voegen* or *passen,* "to fit."

17. Another dubious identification. Smith says a *Dendrobium* sp., only venturing the guess that "it is probably a species of *Dendrobium* of the section *Rhopalanthe*" (M, p. 176).

18. This plant also earns nothing more definite than *Dendrobium* sp. (M, p. 175), though Smith feels that the "description of the flower is strongly suggestive of *Dendrobium confusum* Schltr., but so far as I know Schlechter's species never attains the length noted by Rumphius" (M, p. 175).

19. Seventeenth-century shoes (see page 136, top).

20. Smith (M, p. 173) identifies this plant as *Dendrobium calceolum* Roxb.

Man's shoes from southern Germany; end of seventeenth century.
Bayerisches Nationalmuseum, Munich.

21. The second illustration on plate 51.

22. Smith (M, p. 173) states that the first illustration on plate 51 "can scarcely belong with the plant described as *Herba supplex prima.*" He does not know what plant it might be.

Chapter Ten

1. Original text in II.10.6:112–3.

He means the previous twelve epiphytes.

2. "Standelwort" was "Standel-kruid" in the original, also known as Standergrass in England. Gerard insists these plants were known as "Dogs Stones" (ch. 100, pp. 205–207), that is to say "Dogs' Testicles," due to the shape of the root bulbs. The latter hints that this plant is one of the *Orchidaceae*. "Standelwort" came into English from Middle Dutch, and was a native Dutch name for a local orchid, *Orchis mascula.* The *WNT* reports that there are twenty-eight species of orchids in the Netherlands.

3. Rumphius' "First Terrestrial Orchid" is listed by Smith (M, p. 172) as *Spathoglottis plicata* Blume.

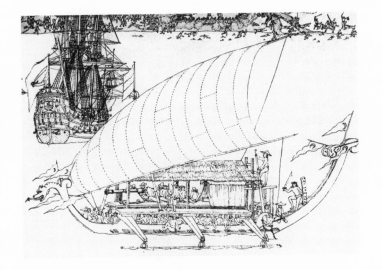

4. A *kora kora* was a vessel particular to the Moluccas. It was in essence a large *orembaai* with very big outriggers. These boats had a wide beam, with an ample amount of space, and very high, decorated stem and stern. In the center was a covered platform. The kora kora was propelled by a large number of oarsmen, sometimes as many as two hundred; some even sat on the wide outriggers. It could carry sail, but no more than one *tanja* sail (a canted rectangular sail) on a tripod mast. With a stiff wind, that sail became a liability because the kora kora was not very seaworthy, and many of them foundered. They were armed with small-caliber ordnance and with sidearms. The oarsmen rowed to the rhythm of *tifa* drums and gongs. In the first half of the seventeenth century, the VOC assembled fleets of kora kora to conduct *hongi* raids, armed naval patrols intended to ensure that the Company's monopoly of the spice trade was maintained and honored. In the second half of the same century, when hostilities had largely ceased, the yearly kora kora fleets were launched primarily for show. These large vessels no longer exist.

5. Probably *Curcuma petiolata* (M, p. 163). Rumphius discusses nine

forms of Curcuma (a kind of curry plant) in 8.16.5:62–168. The "Curcuma Silvestris" or "wild curcuma" is mentioned on pp. 164–165.

6. A yam, *Dioscorea esculenta*, described by Rumphius in 11.13.5:357–359.

7. "Acquelyen" in the original, a bizarre spelling of *akelei*, Dutch for the Columbine flower (*Aquilegia vulgaris* L.). This flower was the symbolic emblem of many *rederijkkamers*, literary clubs of rhetoricians, in seventeenth-century Holland.

8. "Tydeloze" in the original, *tijdeloos* in more modern Dutch. It was more often spelled *tijloos*, and originated in Middle Dutch. It literally means "timeless" and referred to a flower that bloomed at an unusual time, for instance, in very early spring. Although at least five different species of plants were called such, the most common plant with which the term was associated was *Colchicum autumnale* L. or Meadow Saffron, a most remarkable plant for temperate climes in that it produces leaves in spring and seed pods in summer, and it blooms in autumn. Gerard describes these flowers extensively in 1.91.157–164.

9. "Kropgans" in the original. A compound noun assembled from *krop* (crop) and *gans* (goose). Burman was fooled and translated this bird with *anseris*, which means "goose" in Latin, but then he probably never saw a pelican.

10. See n. 15 of ch. 1.

11. Smith (M, pp. 171–172) assigns it *Phaius gratus* Blume. He is unsure of his classification because "this species is unknown to me" (M, p. 171).

12. "Tuber" for *knol*, a rather generic term in Dutch. "Tuber" did not enter the language until the latter half of the seventeenth century but, even if not frequent usage, it is appropriate here because Rumphius distinguishes between this outgrowth and a root.

13. See ch. 1.

14. The Latin means the "First Purple or White Terrestrial Orchid."

15. Misspelling of "kora kora."

16. *Tanah* means land, earth, soil (also in a figurative sense), hence this phrase means "Earth Orchid."

17. This plant is not an orchid, but a member of the Amaryllidaceae: Merrill (M, pp. 142–143) calls it *Curculigo capitulata* (Lour.) Kuntze., and De Wit (p. 87) *Molineria capitulata* (Lour.) Herb.; hence the Ambonese were wrong.

18. Rumphius also spells this Ambonese grass "Hulang" and describes it in 10.14.6:19. Merrill (M, p. 88) lists it as *Andropogon amboinicus* (L.) Merr.

19. Not identified.

20. "Saguer" or "saguire" or "sagwire" is the palm wine called "toddy" by British colonials, extracted from the *Arenga pinnata* palm.

21. See plate 52 (top) and n. 30 of ch.1.

22. Rumphius' "First Ground Angrek" or "Angraecum terrestre primum," which Smith lists as *Spathoglottis plicata* Bl., is *not* illustrated here or on any other plate in the *Herbal*. According to Smith (M, pp. 171–172) the first figure on plate 52 depicts *Phaius amboinensis* Bl., which is described in the next chapter.

23. Figure 3 on plate 50 is (M, p. 171) *Phaius gratus* Bl. or what Rumphius called in the present chapter his "second kind," "Angraecum terrestre primum album."

24. Figure 2 on plate 52 is the orchid described as "Flos triplicatus" in ch. 13, *Calanthe triplicata* (Willemet) Ames.

Chapter Eleven

1. Original text in 11.11.6:113–114.

The Pinang is the fruit of the well-known *Areca catechu* palm, described in 1.5.1:26–31.

2. *Veratrum*, according to De Wit (p. 88).

3. A genus of tropical herbs of the family Zingiberaceae, which includes turmeric. This species is described by Rumphius in 8.16.5:162–168.

4. Smith (M, pp. 170–171) argues that this "Other Ground Orchid" is *Phaius amboinensis* Bl.

5. Indonesian for "Ground Orchid."

6. This is *incorrect*. The present orchid, *Phaius amboinensis* Bl., is depicted on plate 52, fig. 1. Fig. 3 on plate 50 shows *Phaius gratus* Bl.

7. *Hortus Malabaricus,* vol. 11, pp. 69–70, fig. 35.

8. This refers to the commentary Caspar Commelin added to the entries in the *Hortus Malabaricus* in his text: Commelin, *Flora Malabarica.*

9. Perhaps Burman is referring here to his own work: Joan Burman, *Flora Malabarica* (Amsterdam, 1769).

10. Plukenet, *Amaltheum Botanicum.*

Chapter Twelve

1. Original text in 11.12.6:114–115.

Merrill (M, pp. 142–143) identifies this as *Curculigo capitulata* (Lour.) Kuntze. The Latin *involucrum* refers to something that is used to wrap things in. This plant is not an orchid but a species of the Amaryllidaceae. Its leaves look like those of orchids.

2. See n. 5 of ch. 10.

3. "Globba" or *galoba* refers to a genus of the Zingiberaceae, described by Rumphius in 11.29–33.6:134–142.

4. "Kolf[ke]" in the original. The word "spike," meaning a form of inflorescence, was current in Rumphius' day. In modern botany this is the spadix.

5. It would seem that Rumphius coined this word himself; at least he states as much in his description of "Lampujang" (*Zingiber* sp.) in 8.10.5:148. The Dutch noun for it, he says, would be "onderwas" or "ondergewas." He derived "Hypophyton" from the Greek verb ὑποφύω, which, according to Liddell and Scott, means "to make to grow from below." What I think he has in mind is "sucker," a word current in the sixteenth century, when it already meant "a shoot thrown out from the base of a tree or plant, which in most cases may serve for propagation; now *esp.* such a shoot rising from the root underground" (*OED*).

6. What he called "Globba durion mera," more commonly *galoba durian merah*, is the plant *Amomum roseum* Roxb. Rumphius discussed the plant in 11.30.6:137–138.

7. "Bonkus," elsewhere spelled "bonckos," are native cigarettes. Rumphius was not familiar with this way of smoking, so he noted it in particular when he discussed the tobacco plant in 8.40.5:225–227. This is how he described them: "After the green leaves [of the tobacco plant] are dried in the wind, and cut into narrow strips, they are wrapped in dry and smoothed Pissang [=banana] leaves, about five to six inches long, and as thick as one's little finger. These small rolls are called *Bonckos* by the Malay, and are lit at their ends, placed in the mouth, and sucked on" (5:225).

8. The seeds of the kanari tree, *Canarium commune* L., an important staple in the Moluccas in Rumphius' day. He described this important tree in 3.1.2:145–150.

9. "Busagtig" in the original, most likely a misprint for "buisachtig," that is, something that is round and hollow.

10. *Amomum cardamomum* Willd., described by Rumphius in 8.12.5:152–153.

Chapter Thirteen

1. Original text in 11.13.6:115–116.
Comber identifies this as *Calanthe triplicata* (Willemet) Ames.

2. See n. 2 of ch.1.

3. *Gentiana* is today the type genus of the Gentianaceae, comprising numerous herbs.

4. "Plantago" normally refers to forms of plantain; *Plantago* is the name of the genus. Henk van der Werff informed me that the reason for Rumphius' comparison is that "orchids have leaves with parallel venation, that is to say, their leaves have several veins of more or less equal thickness which run from the base to the tip of the leaf parallel to each other. Plantago has, like many orchids, parallel venation; the lower leaf surface is also ribbed by the raised veins. Hence plantago leaves resemble the leaves of terrestrial orchids in terms of venation and shape."

5.

Zodiacal sign of Aries.

6. "Triple Flower."

7. "Ambonese Hellebore."

8. "Three-layered Flower." *Bunga* is "flower," *tiga* means the number "three," and *lapis* is a "layer" or "stratum" (among other meanings).

9. Stands of *Melaleuca leucadendron* trees, which have a white bark, hence are "bright" ("ligt" in the original) when seen in the otherwise relentlessly green tropical landscape.

10. This fern, listed by Merrill (M, p. 69) as *Gleichenia linearis,* is described by Rumphius in 10.58.6:85–86. He states that people used the black stems of these ferns instead of goose quills when writing Arabic script, because they were firmer.

11. "Bangle" is *banglai* or *banglé,* a ginger, *Zingiber cassumunar,* described by Rumphius in 8.13.5:154–155.

12. De Wit (p. 90) says this is *Syzygium aromaticum,* i.e., the clove tree.

13. The betel-nut palm, *Areca catechu* L.

Chapter Fourteen

1. Original text in 11.14.6:116–117.
See n. 2 of ch. 1.

2. "Orchis" was first used by Theophrastus, and thereafter by other classical botanists such as Hippocrates, Dioscorides, Galen, and Pliny. *Orchis* is now a genus of European terrestrial orchids, comprising some thirty-five species.

3. For "standelwort" see n. 2 of ch. 10.

4. Described in 8.70.5:286–288. Included here following ch. 15.

5. This is *Polianthes tuberosa* L. and described in 8.69.5:285–286. It was cultivated specifically for its marvelous scent.

6. Rumphius' Latin phrase means: "Large Ambonese Orchid, with a root that looks like fingers." This is a species of *Eulophia*, but Smith (M, p. 172) is by no means certain which one.

7. *Spathoglottis plicata* Bl., described in ch. 10, the first kind.

8. "Lampujang," now *lempuyang*, a plant related to ginger. Merrill (M, p. 152) reduced it to *Zingiber zerumbet*, and Rumphius described it in 8.10.5:148–150.

9. This is a coral, *Isis hippuris* L., as identified by Bayer (*MV*, 240). For the comparison see Rumphius' description in 12.16.6:228–232.

10. The Latin phrase means: "Large Ambonese Orchid, with a Root resembling a Radish." This is not an orchid, but, according to Merrill (M, p. 142), *Curculigo orchioides* Gaertn. It is related to what Rumphius called "Involucrum" or "the Wrapper" in ch. 12, and which is *Curculigo capitulata.*

11. Rumphius spells this strange phrase "tommon contsji" in the title of his chapter describing it, in 8.18.5:172–173. Now spelled *temu kunci*, this medicinal plant is listed by most as *Gastrochilus pandurata* (Roxb.) Ridl., but Merrill (M, p. 162) reduces it to *Kaempferia pandurata* Roxb.

12. "Satyrium" is an ancient name associated with orchid species, derived from "Satyr" because of the plant's alleged erotic powers. In

1800, Olof Swartz made *Satyrium* the name "of a genus of European terrestrial orchids" (Lawler, p. 43).

13. As before, this merely means "Ground Orchid."

14. I think "alea" is *halia*, the Indonesian word for ginger.

15. *Hitam* means "black."

16. For "lugtig."

17. "Snygras" in the original. This refers to the well-known, but infamous *alang-alang* grass, a very sharp grass that will cut travellers traversing the sometimes large expanses of it. It is a species of *Imperata*.

18. *Ubi* is a general word for tubers, but Rumphius probably had in mind the yam he called the "common ubi" or "Ubium vulgare," in 9.7.5:346–349. Merrill lists it as *Dioscorea alata* L. (M, p. 146).

19. "Combili" or kombili, is an edible tuber, *Dioscorea esculenta*, described by Rumphius in 9.13.5:357–359.

20. "Bernsteen" in the original. The Dutch noun *bernsteen* refers only to the fossil resin that is the true Baltic amber, not to the substance obtained from the sperm whale; see *ACC*, p. 499, n. 1.

21. "Apostematie" in the original, which was an inflated synonym for *aposteem*, and meant the same thing: abscess or pustule.

22. In the original "negen-ogen," which literally translates as "nine eyes"—a nasty boil, called such, it seems, because it often begins as a number of small pimples.

23. "Buro malacco" was the Ternatan name of the plant Rumphius called "Oculus astaci" or, in Malay, "Matta udan," that is to say "Shrimp eye," and described in 9.82.5:479. Merrill lists it as *Cissus aristata* Bl. (M, p. 344).

24. That is to say, the plant that belongs to the Amaryllidaceae, *Curculigo orchioides.*

25. The orchid *Habenaria rumphii*, discussed in the next chapter.

26. A form of the orchid genus *Peristylus*, for which see the next chapter.

Chapter Fifteen

1. Original text in 11.15.6:118–119.

Smith (M, p. 169) lists this orchid as *Habenaria rumphii* (Brongn.) Lindl. This is the same plant as the *second* one (the "little orchid") mentioned in the next chapter, entitled "The Susanna Flower" (from 8.70.5:287).

2. That is to say the orchid inflorescence, which is usually a raceme. We associate this noun mostly with corn, but that is not intended here. Rumphius means a "spike" of flowers. The original word was "air," variant spelling of *aar*, the spike or head of European cereal plants.

3. For "weinig."

4. The edible tuber *Dioscorea esculenta.*

5. To indicate the seasons in tropical regions is tricky because of the great variability in wind direction and geographical features. I think one might safely say that the tropical year is roughly divided into three periods. The "wet" or East monsoon in Rumphius' region appears to be from May to August, with September and October as the transition months to the "dry" or West monsoon, which is roughly from November to February, with March and April as the transition months to the wet monsoon. This division would be different in other parts of the archipelago, in some places the exact opposite. For instance, on Java, the dry monsoon is from May to August, with September and October as the *kentering* months to the wet monsoon, which is from November to February, with March and April as the *kentering* months to the dry season again. The four transition months (another nice expression for them was *twijfelmaanden* or "indecisive months"), March, April, September, and October, are called the *kentering* in Dutch, a very specific term not encountered for this purpose in other languages. *Kenteren* is clearly related to the verb *kantelen,* to turn over. *Kantelen* was originally used for the time period when the tides change. Those *kentering* months can cover a shorter time, seldom longer. Generally speaking, April and October are the inevitable *kentering* months in the Indian Ocean. That period was also the most

perilous for one's health and notorious for a higher incidence of death than at any other time of the year. This is true for the rest of Asia and for Africa as well. See Ludeking, "Schets," p. 18.

On this basis, one would have to say that this orchid blooms, roughly, sometime between August and November.

6. The Latin means simply "Small Ambonese Orchid."

7. The Malay is even simpler: "Small Orchid."

8. See n. 17 in ch. 14.

9. "Red Mountain" or *Batu merah* was a hill northeast of Victoria Castle, the VOC's main fortress in the region. The Batu merah district was Muslim.

10. This "second kind" is, according to Smith (M, p. 169), a species of *Peristylus*, but he does "not know any species like it from Amboina." De Wit (p. 93) ventures the guess *Peristylus goodyeroides* (D. Don) Lindl.

11. This stem is a maximum of 9 1/2 inches.

12. Eight inches of bare stem.

13. Just over half an inch.

14. See ch. 9.

15. For the original "stam" which normally, in modern Dutch, means "trunk" and is commonly not used for a part of a flower or plant. But in Dutch botanical literature *stam* (*truncus* in Latin) very specifically refers to woody stems of plants which live longer than one year, while the stem of a plant that lives only for one blooming season is called a *stengel* (*caulis* in Latin), according to the *WNT*, under *stam*. Since Rumphius had not used it before in this orchid context, I kept it, thinking he had this specific meaning in mind.

16. Jacob Breyne, *Exoticarum aliarumque minus cognitarum Plantarum Centuria Prima* (Danzig, 1678).

17. See n. 64 of ch. 1.

18. See n. 65 of ch. 1.

19. *Hortus Malabaricus*, vol. 12, pp. 53–54, fig. 27.

The Susanna Flower

1. Original text in 8.70.5:286–288.

This is *Pecteilis susannae* (R.Br.) Raf. as identified by Comber, *Orchids of Java*, p. 67.

2. Throughout Rumphius' writings on orchids, "orchis," "orchides," "satyria," and "angrec" (now *anggrek*) are synonyms.

3. See n. 44 of ch. 1. The reference is most likely to *Stirpium historiae pemptakes sex sive libri XXX* (Antwerp: Plantijn, 1583, 1616).

In the contemporary English translation of Dodoens' herbal, orchids are discussed in book 2, ch. 51 (pp. 245–251), under the name of "Standelwort" or "Standergrass." He distinguishes five kinds: 1) "Cynosorchin, sive canis testiculum," 2) "Testiculum Morionis," 3) "Tragorchin," 4) "Orchin Serapian," and 5) "Testiculum odoratum or Testiculum pumilionem." The plant with which Rumphius compares his "Flos Susannae" is described as having leaves that are somewhat long, broad, and smooth, and a stalk that is "a foote long, on which groweth here and there in a spikie bush on top, certain pleasant white floures, somewhat like Butterflies with a little taile hanging behind, in which is a certaine sweete juice or moisture like honie in taste." Quoted from Dodoens, *A New Herball*, p. 248. See also, Jacquet, pp. 33–102.

4. "Weegbere" in the original, which should be *weegbree*, plants of the genus *Plantago*. It is difficult to say if Rumphius is referring to the European plantain or to the plant he considered a tropical variety. He called it "Plantago aquatica" or "Water Lettuce" (11.53.6:177–178) which Merrill, (M, p. 132) identified as *Pistia stratiotes* L.

5. Latinization of the Indonesian name for the orchid: *anggrek*.

6. *Bunga* is the general Indonesian word for flower, while it is also used in a variety of wonderful phrases meaning "the flowering of something," for instance *bunga api* or "fire flower" (a spark or fireworks); *musim bunga* or "flower season" (spring); *bunga karang* or "flower of the coral reef" (sponge); *bunga* can also mean interest on one's money, the "flowering" of one's money.

7. This appears to be the only mention we have of Rumphius' first wife; I have been unable to discover anything else. We know only her

first name, and I do not even know for sure that Rumphius was married to Susanna. The word that refers to her in this moving sentence is "Gezellinne," which in a general sense meant "companion" but also could specifically refer to a man's spouse. And yet, at the time the noun *huisvrouw* was a more common and legal locution for one's wife. The fact that only her first or Christian name is given might suggest that she was not Dutch but a local woman.

8. This means "earth orchid," in Indonesian, that is to say, one of the terrestrial orchids.

9. The southern peninsula of the two that together form the island of Ambon.

10. *Melaleuca leucadendron* L. is the tree that produces the essential oil, distilled from its leaves, known as cajeput oil. Rumphius was the first to describe the tree and its product: 2. 25–26.2:72–77. In the Moluccas the island of Buru was particularly known for the production of cajeput oil; see the fine novel by Beb Vuyk entitled *Het laatste huis van de wereld* (1939). It was translated by André Lefevere with the title *The Last House in the World* and published in *Two Tales of the East Indies* (Amherst: University of Massachusetts Press, 1983).

11. In his *Flora of Manila*, Merrill spells it *Macabuhay* and identifies it as *Tinospora reticulata*. It is a climbing vine with pale-green flowers indigenous to the Philippines, where it blooms from March to May. See Merrill, *A Flora of Manila*, p. 204.

12. This "little orchid" is *Habenaria rumphii* (Brongn.) Lindl., and is described at length by Rumphius in 11.15.6:118–119. See previous chapter.

13. Rumphius includes many references to China in his work, both scholarly and based on personal communication. As to the first, he uses most frequently a once celebrated work by the Italian priest Martinus Martini (1614–1661), entitled *Novus atlas Sinensis*, published in Amsterdam in 1655, commonly referred to as "Atlas Sinensis." Martini had been a Catholic missionary in China, so that his writing was based in fact. Rumphius most likely encountered Martini's work in the substantial borrowings made by Martini's teacher, Athanasius Kircher (1602–1680), mentioned in the first chapter. Kircher included Martini's information

in his famous *China illustrata*, published in Amsterdam in 1667. Kircher never went to Asia.

Rumphius' other source for Chinese information was a substantial Chinese emigrant population in the island's capital, Kota Ambon. Towards the end of Rumphius' century, the total number of the town's citizens was not quite six thousand. In 1673, for instance, VOC personnel, including their families, numbered 1,198, with 748 other Europeans. But there were also 967 Chinese citizens. See Knaap, "A City of Migrants," *Indonesia* (1991), 105–128, esp. p. 119. According to Rumphius' own testimony (6:122), these Chinese people largely emigrated to the Indies from southern China, particularly from the two coastal provinces of Guangdong (formerly romanized as "Kuangtun," and spelled "Quantung" by Rumphius) and Fujian (formerly Fukien, spelled "Fockien" by Rumphius). Whenever Rumphius quotes Chinese that is not from printed sources, it is a southern dialect form.

It is, therefore, quite normal to find a Chinese reference in his work; the surprise is that there were no others in his orchid texts, especially when one knows that the earliest records about orchids are alleged to come from China. The controversy about the first confirmed mention of orchids in Chinese literature does not concern us here, but there seems to be some consensus that the first specific literary mention of orchids is from the Han period (about 206 B.C. to A.D. 220; see Lawler, pp. 30–31). Needham (*Science and Civilization in China*, vol. 6, part 1, p. 418) asserts that the "first of the monographs consecrated entirely to orchids was produced . . . by Chao Shih-Kêng, a ninth-generation descendant of the imperial house, who conceived a passion for these plants and wrote in +1233 his *Chin-Chang Lan Phu* (A Treatise on the Orchids of Fukien). . . ." Fukien was the home territory of some of the Ambonese Chinese, and that they might have seen a resemblance to a Chinese plant is not surprising considering the fact, noted by Chen and Tang, that "the orchid flora of southern China is closely related to that of Malaysia." Chen and Tang concluded that there are "158 genera and 966 species in China, 82 genera and 550 species are terrestrials, and 64 genera and 416 species are epiphytes. The remaining 17 genera and 33 species are 'saprophytes'" (Chen, pp. 72–73).

It is difficult if not impossible to be absolutely certain which Chinese plant Rumphius has in mind. This, and many other seventeenth-century printed texts, had several layers of obfuscation built in where foreign languages were concerned. In Rumphius' case there was, first, a contemporary phonetic approximation of the informant's pronunciation, second, the transcription of that oral estimate by a scribe ignorant of the language, and, finally, the inevitable misprints of the already dubious product on the printed page—a nightmare for editors and commentators.

In this case we have "Pu Sang-Tjan," which Rumphius translates as meaning either "mother without child, or child without mother," in other words an orphan.

14. Paul Hermann (1646–1695) obtained a medical degree at Padua in 1670. From 1672 to 1680 he worked as a botanist for the VOC on Ceylon; subsequently he became professor of botany at the University of Leiden and director of its botanical garden. The cited work is Hermann, *Paradisus Batavus.*

15. Plukenet, *Almagesti.* The sentence is not clear in the original.

The Petola Leaf

1. The original text was 10.64.6:93–94. The other important item is plate 41, which appeared at 10.63.6:92, the end of ch. 63.

Smith (M, p. 169) identifies the orchid that is described as *Anoectochilus reinwardtii* Blume. It is depicted, according to Smith, on plate 41, fig. 3. Smith thinks that figure 2 on plate 41 might represent *Zeuxine amboinensis* (J. J. Sm.) Schltr. Rumphius did not describe it, and Smith adds that the illustration shows a sterile plant (M, p. 169).

2. In his text, Rumphius seems to say they are the same; see 10.17.6:24.

3. I think he says this because this species of *Commelina* "lies with its green, soft, and round stems on the ground" (6:23).

4. I think he is referring to *Commelina benghalensis* L., as Merrill has it (M, p. 134), although Rumphius did not give it a specific name before (see 6:24).

5. *Begonia tuberosa* Lam. according to Merrill (M, p. 379). Described by Rumphius in 9.70.5:457–458. The connection is once again that it "creeps with its round, and fat stems, which are not very long, over rocks, or along the ground" (5:457). Its fruit is described the same way as the orchid's.

6. The Latin means the "Petola Leaf [or Plant]," and the Malay means the same thing.

7. The word "petola" or "patola" presents something of a problem in orchid lore. Rumphius' name survived in the label *Macodes petola*, but Smith is adamant that Rumphius' orchid "Folium petolatum" is not the same plant (M, p. 169). However, the word "petola" has inspired some strange tales. In a recent popular text (Berliocchi, *The Orchid in Lore and Legend*, p. 102) it is stated that *Macodes petola* comes from the Javanese vernacular and "means letter paper. Its leaves are covered in a network of metallic veins bearing an extraordinary resemblance to the script of its native land, so much so that Rumphius adopted the name as long ago as 1750 [*sic!*], calling this orchid Folium petolatum in his *Herbarium Amboinense*." Lawler (p. 40) also says that this plant was "called 'letter leaf' because the leaf markings were held to resemble Javanese letter symbols" (see also n. 18 on that same p. 40). Now the leaves of this orchid have these markings:

Photograph courtesy of J. B. Comber.

Javanese script (either Kawi or more modern and not romanised) looks like this:

ꦍ ꦎ ꦏ ꦐ ꦑ ꦒ ꦓ ꦔ ꦕ	ꦖ ꦗ ꦘ ꦙ ꦚ
ꦛ ꦜ ꦝ ꦞ ꦟ ꦠ	ꦡ ꦢ ꦣ
ꦤ ꦥ ꦦ ꦧ ꦨ ꦩ ꦪ ꦫ ꦬ	ꦭ ꦮ ꦯ ꦰ
ꦱ ꦲ ꦳ ꦴ ꦵ ꦶ ꦷ ꦸ ꦹ	ꦺ ꦻ ꦼ ꦽ
ꦾ ꦿ ꧀ ꧁ ꧂ ꧃ ꧄ ꧅ ꧆	꧇ ꧈ ꧉ ꧊ ꧋

Source: Raffles, *The History of Java*, vol. 2: plate opposite p. 370. This script looks more like the markings of *Grammatophyllum scriptum* pictured in ch. 1 than the present orchid's leaves.

One might dismiss this as a judgment call, but there is still the word *petola* or *patola* itself. Horne's *Javanese-English Dictionary* glosses *patola* as "a fine soft silk material," but does not say anything about its decorative patterns. Wilkinson's *Malay-English Dictionary* lists it under Rumphius' spelling as *petola*, gives as its first meaning: "brightly marked," and goes on "of gaily colored cloths described by old writers as 'Indian coloured cottons and silks much prized at Malacca'." Hence the word chiefly refers to what was originally a woven pattern in cloth, specifically silk. This cloth was very desirable and expensive, which can be ascertained from invoices printed by De Haan of lists of textiles given as presents to Javanese aristocracy in 1714. Petola silk (spelled "patholen zijde") is invariably the most expensive textile item. See De Haan, 2:419–422. Wilkinson states that *petola* (patola) is a word from Malayalam, a language from the Dravidian family, spoken on India's western coast, which contains many Sanskrit words. This was the language of the Brahmins Van Reede tot Drakenstein recorded in his *Hortus Malabaricus*. In the seventeenth century, most of India's piece-goods (as the British called them) were shipped from that coast. Hence one can safely say that *petola* or *patola* never had any association with orthography, but always referred to a textile pattern. "Patola" derives from Sanskrit *pata*, which the *Sanskrit-English Dictionary* glosses as "woven cloth," "cloth," "a painted piece of cloth." See Monier-Williams, *Sanskrit-English Dictionary*.

This silk cloth was not a common commodity but quite familiar to

Patola cloth from Gujarat in India.
Silk, double ikat, from the end of the nineteenth century.
39676/ 66187 Collection Wereldmuseum Rotterdam.

the higher VOC officials, as the De Haan entry proves. Rumphius was
well acquainted with it as well, as the quote in the present chapter tes-
tifies. And there are other contexts; for instance, in 9.42–45.5:405–410,
he devotes considerable space to descriptions of species of dishcloth
gourds (*Luffa*), all of which he labels under the sort-name "Petola" because "of the resemblance of the gourds to a particular silk cloth, called
such, that is painted with various flowers, figures, and spots" (5:405).
In 1.2.1:15, he mentions that a large snake prefers to live in the top
of coconut palms. He calls it *Ular Pethola* (note the same spelling that
De Haan transcribed) and writes that he does so because it is "beautifully covered with patches of white and black, with a little yellow
mixed in, almost like a silken cloth called Pethola." The snake is the
large *Python reticulatus*. Then there is a shell which Rumphius named

"Cochlea petholata" in Latin and "Bia pethola" in Malay, now considered a turbo shell, *Turbo petholatus* L. Rumphius writes that he gave it that name because it is "decorated in several colors, like *Pethola* cloths, or the large *Ular pethola* Snake" (*ACC*, p. 101).

An orchid, gourds, a snake, and a shell all share the sobriquet *petola* because their markings resembled a woven pattern in a familiar cloth, *not* a highly sophisticated script known only to a small intellectual elite. By the way, Lawler prints a totally different version of why *Macodes patola* was called such (one that tallies with my argument) on p. 41:

> The Javanese regard this plant as of divine origin and relate the following legend: Long ago a radiantly beautiful goddess, Petola, was sent by the gods to Java to show the uncivilized natives the right and good ways. Her gentleness did not persuade them, and they chased her away to a rocky outcrop in the deep forest. She returned the next day in an angry mood and the people then subjected themselves to her. They pleaded for her beautiful scarf as a sign of her forgiveness, but she could not leave it. She returned to the rocky outcrop and while asleep laid her scarf on the ground. Soon the ground was covered with lovely plants that bore on their leaves the pattern of the heavenly scarf; and so originated the *daun petola* of Java, brought there by a goddess. Soon the news of the divine flowers spread, and people came from far and near to collect them for themselves. All these plants, however, began to die. The goddess magically restored them to the rock, breathed life into them, and left them in the care of the mountain fairies. The Javanese explain that this is why the plant cannot be grown away from the place of its origin.

I should note that Berliocchi mentions Rumphius prominently but inadequately in several places in *The Orchid in Lore and Legend*. His biographical sketch (pp. 41–42) is full of errors: for instance, Rumphius obviously completed his *Herbal before* his death (one could even say that the "Auctuarium," or seventh volume, was merely a volume of addenda); in its final form the work was in six volumes plus the "Auctuarium" (or volume seven), *not* "twelve," and by no stretch of the imagination can it be said that "two of [the twelve volumes] are devoted to orchids" (p. 42), as the present work clearly indicates. The orchid chapters are part only of book eleven in volume six, with a couple of chapters scattered in other "books" in other volumes. On p. 100 Berliocchi prints a picture of *Pecteilis susannae*, and has no idea that Rumphius was the first to describe it and that he named it after his (presumed) wife. On p. 151 a statement about *Phalaenopsis* should be emended to read that Rumphius was the *first* botanist to describe any species of this genus. And so on.

8. "Widely spaced" for the troublesome locution *ydel*, which, I think, here means that those trees do not grow close together.

9. This passage is very important. It proves that Rumphius did produce his own illustrations before he became blind, either in pen and ink or in watercolor. Secondly, he also seems to have assembled a herbarium of sorts, either in its own right, or as adjunct samples, as was the case here. Hence we can say for sure that the original illustrations for this *Herbal* were made by Rumphius and that they were destroyed in the fire that on January 11, 1687, burned down the European quarters of Kota Ambon, the island's capital, including Rumphius' house and belongings.

BIBLIOGRAPHY

Arditti, Joseph. *Fundamentals of Orchid Biology.* New York: John Wiley, 1992.

———. "Caproic Acid in Satyrium Flowers: Biochemical Origins of a Myth." *American Orchid Society Bulletin* 41 (April 1972): 298–300.

———, ed. *Orchid Biology. Reviews and Perspectives.* Eight volumes. Several publishers, 1977–2001.

Arditti, Joseph, and Abdul Karim Abdul Ghani. "Numerical and Physical Properties of Orchid Seeds and Their Biological Implications." *New Phytology* 45 (2000): *367–421.*

Beehler, Bruce M., Thane K. Pratt, and Dale A. Zimmerman. *Birds of New Guinea.* Princeton: Princeton University Press, 1986.

Berliocchi, Luigi. *The Orchid in Lore and Legend.* Trans. Lenore Rosenberg and Anita Weston. Portland, Ore.: Timber Press, 2000.

Bontius, J. "Historiae Naturalis & Medicae Liber Sextus. De Plantis, & Aromatibus." In Gulielmi Pisonis, *De Indiae Utriusque Re naturali et Medica.* Amsterdam: Elzevier, 1658.

Breyne, Jacob. *Exoticarum aliarumque minus cognitarum Plantarum Centuria Prima.* Danzig, 1678.

Burman, Joan. *Flora Malabarica.* Amsterdam, 1769.

Chan, C. L., A. Lamb, P. S. Shin, and J. J. Wood. *Orchids of Borneo, Vol. I, Introduction and a Selection of Species.* Orchids of Borneo. Sabah, Malaysia: The Sabah Society, 1994.

Chandler, Raymond. *Stories and Early Novels.* The Library of America. New York: Literary Classics of the United States, Inc., 1995.

Chase, M. W., J. V Freudenstein, and K. M. Cameron, "DNA Data and Orchidaceae Systematics: A New Phylogenetic Classification." *The First International Orchid Conservation Congress Incorporating the 2nd International Orchid Population Biology Conference.* Perth, 2001.

Chen Sing-Chi and Tang Tsin. "A General Review of the Orchid Flora of China." *Orchid Biology. Reviews and Perspectives, II.* Ed. Joseph Arditti. Ithaca, N.Y.: Cornell University Press, 1982.

Clercq, F. S. A. de. *Nieuw Plantkundig Woordenboek voor Nederlandsch Indië.* 2d rev. ed. Amsterdam: J. H. de Bussy, 1927.

Clusius, Carolus. *Rariorum plantarum historia.* Antwerp: Plantin, 1601.

Coates, Brian J., and K. David Bishop. *A Guide to the Birds of Wallacea, Sulawesi, the Moluccas, and Lesser Sunda Islands.* Alderley: Dove, 1997.

Comber, J. B. *Orchids of Java.* London: Royal Botanic Gardens, Kew, 1990.

Commelin, Caspar. *Flora Malabarica sive Horti Malabarici Catalogus Exhibens Omnium ejusdem Plantarum nomina.* Leiden, 1696.

Crown, Alan. "Samaritan Miniscule Palaeography." *Bulletin of the John Rylands University Library of Manchester* 63 (2) (Spring 1981): 330–368.

Dodoens, D. Rembert. *A New Herball, or Historie of Plants.* Translated from French into English by Henrie Lyte. London: Edm. Bollifant, 1595.

Dressler, Robert L. *The Orchids: Natural History and Classification* [1981]. Reprint ed., Cambridge: Harvard University Press, 1990.

————. *Phylogeny and Classification of the Orchid Family.* Portland, Ore.: Dioscorides Press, 1993.

Dupperes, Aloys. *Orchids of Europe.* 1955. Trans. A. J. Huxley. London: Blandford Press, 1961.

Flora Europea. Vol. 5: Alismataceae to Orchidaceae (Monocotyledones). Ed. T. G. Tutin. Cambridge: Cambridge University Press, 1980.

Gerard, John. *The Herbal or General History of Plants* [1633]. Revised and Enlarged by Thomas Johnson. Reprint ed., New York: Dover, 1975.

Gessner, Conrad. *Historia plantarum et vires ex Dioscoride, paulo Aegineta, Theophrasto, Plinio, & recentioribus Graecis, juxta elementorum ordinem.* Basil: Robertum Wynter, 1541.

The Greek Herbal of Dioscorides, Illustrated by a Byzantine. A.D. 512. Trans. John Goodyear, 1655. Edited and First Printed 1933 by Robert T. Gunther. Oxford: Oxford University Press, 1934.

Haan, F. de. *Priangan. De Preanger-Regentschappen onder het Nederlandsch Bestuur tot 1811.* 4 vols. Batavia: Bataviaasch Genootschap van Kunsten en Wetenschappen, 1910–1912.

Hansen, Eric. *Orchid Fever: A Horticultural Tale of Love, Lust, and Lunacy.* New York: Pantheon, 2000.

Heniger, J. *Hendrik Adriaan van Reede tot Drakenstein (1636–1691) and Hortus Malabaricus: A Contribution to the History of Dutch Colonial Botany.* Rotterdam: A. A. Balkema, 1986.

Hermann, Paul. *Paradisus Batavus, Continens Plus centum Plantas affabrè aere incisas & Descriptionibus illustras.* Leiden, 1698.

Heyne, K. *De Nuttige Planten van Nederlandsch Indië.* 2d rev. ed., 2 vols. Batavia: Department van Landbouw, Nijverheid & Handel in Nederlandsch-Indië, 1927.

Horne, Elinor Clark. *Javanese-English Dictionary.* New Haven: Yale University Press, 1974.

Jacquet, Pierre. "History of Orchids in Europe, from Antiquity to the 17th Century." *Orchid Biology. Reviews and Perspectives, VI.* Ed. Joseph Arditti. New York: John Wiley & Sons, 1994.

Kircher, Athanasius. *Mundus subterraneus, in XII libros digestus; quo divinum subterrestris mundi opificium, mira ergasteriorum naturae in eo distributio, verbo pant' amorphou Protei regnum, universae denique naturae majestas & divitiae summa rerum varietate exponuntur.* Amsterdam: J. Janssonium & E. Weyerstraten, 1665.

Knaap, Gerrit J. "A City of Migrants: Kota Ambon at the End of the Seventeenth Century." *Indonesia,* no. 51 (April 1991).

Lawler, Leonard J. "Ethnobotany of the Orchidaceae." *Orchid Biology. Reviews and Perspectives, III.* Ed. Joseph Arditti. Ithaca, N.Y.: Cornell University Press, 1984.

Leupe, P. A. "Georgius Everhardus Rumphius, Ambonsch Natuurkundige der zeventiende eeuw." *Verhandelingen der Koninklijke Akademie van Wetenschappen* 12:1–63. Amsterdam: C. G. van der Post, 1871.

Lewis, Charlton T., and Charles Short. *A Latin Dictionary.* Oxford: Clarendon Press, 1879.

Lewis, Martha W. Hoffman. "Power and Passion: The Orchid in Literature." *Orchid Biology. Reviews and Perspectives, V.* Ed. Joseph Arditti. Portland, Ore.: Timber Press, 1990.

Ludeking, E. W. A. "Schets van de Residentie Amboina." In *Bijdragen tot de Taal-Land-en Volkenkunde van Nederlandsch Indië,* derde volgreeks, derde deel 1868.

Martini, Martinus. *China illustrata.* Amsterdam, 1667.

———. *Novus atlas Sinensis.* Amsterdam, 1655.

Merrill, E. D. *A Flora of Manila.* Manila: Bureau of Scientific Publications, 1912.

———. *An Interpretation of Rumphius's Herbarium Amboinense.* Manila: Bureau of Printing, 1917.

Millar, Andrée. *Orchids of Papua New Guinea.* Portland, Ore.: Timber Press, 1999.

Miscellanea Curiosa sive Ephemeridum Medico-Physicarum Germanicarum Academiae Imperialis Leopoldinae Naturae Curiosorum. Nuremberg: Wolfgang Maurit Endter, 1683.

Monier-Williams, Monier. *Sanskrit-English Dictionary* [1899]. Reprint ed., Oxford: Clarendon Press, 1970.

Needham, Joseph. *Science and Civilisation in China.* 7 vols. in 11 parts. Vol. 6: *Biology and Biological Technology.* Part 1: Botany. Cambridge: Cambridge University Press, 1986.

O'Byrne, P. *Lowland Orchids of Papua New Guinea.* Singapore: SNP Publishers, 1994.

Ordoño, Cesar Macazaga. *Diccionario de la Lengua Nahuatl.* México, D.F.: Editorial Innovación, 1981.

Orlean, Susan. *The Orchid Thief.* New York: Ballantine Books, 1998.

Oxford English Dictionary. 17 vols. Oxford: Oxford University Press, 1933.

Pausanias. *Description of Greece.* Trans. W. H. S. Jones, H. A. Ormerod, and R. E. Wycherley. 5 vols. London: Heinemann, 1918–1935.

Pisonis, Gulielmi. *De Indiae Utriusque, Re naturali et Medica.* Amsterdam: Elzevier, 1658.

Pliny. *Natural History.* Trans. H. Rackham, W. H. S. Jones, and E. Eichholz. 10 vols. Loeb Classical Library. Cambridge: Harvard University Press, 1938–1962.

Plukenet, Leonard. *Almagestum Botanicum sive Phytographiae Pluc'netianae Onomasticon Methodo Syntheticâ digestum.* London, 1696.

———. *Almagesti Botanici Mantissa.* London: 1705.

———. *Amaltheum Botanicum.* London, 1705.

———. *Phytographia, sive Stirpium Illustriorum & minus cognitarum Icones.* London, 1691.

Proust, Marcel. *A la Recherche du Temps Perdu.* 3 vols. Bibliothèque de la Pléiade. Paris: Gallimard, 1954.

Raffles, Thomas Stamford. *The History of Java.* 2 vols. [1817]. Reprint ed., Kuala Lumpur: Oxford University Press, 1978.

Recchi, Nardo Antonio. *Rerum medicarum Nouae Hispaniae thesaurus, seu, Plantarum animalium mineralium mexicanorum historia.* Rome: Vitalis Mascardi, 1651.

Reinikka, Merle. *A History of the Orchid.* Coral Gables, Fla.: University of Miami Press, 1972.

Royen, P. van. *The Orchids of the High Mountains of New Guinea.* Hirschberg: Strauss & Cramer, 1979.

Rumphius, Georgius Everhardus. *Het Amboinsche Kruid-boek. Dat is, Beschryving van de meest bekende Boomen, Heesters, Kruiden, Land- en Water-Planten, die men in Amboina, en de omleggende eylanden vind, Na haare gedaante, verscheide benamingen, aanqueking, en gebruik: mitsgaders van eenige insecten en gediertens, Voor 't meeste deel met de Figuren daar toe behoorende, Allen met veel moeite en vleit in veele jaaren vergadert, en beschreven in twaalf boeken, door Georgius Everhardus Rumphius, Med. Doct. van Hanau, Oud Koopman en Raadsperoon in Amboina, mitsgaders onder de naam van Plinius Indicus, Lid van de Illustre Academia Naturae Curiosorum, in 't Duitsche en Roomsche Ryk opgerigt. Nagezien en uitgegeven door Joannes Burmannus, Med. Doct. en Botanices Professor in den Hortus Medicus te Amsterdam, Medelidt van het Keyzerlyke Queekschool der onderzoekers van de Natuurkunde; Die daar ver-*

scheide Benamingen, en zyne Aanmerkingen heeft bygevoegt. 6 vols. Amsterdam, By François Changuion, Jan Catuffe, Hermanus Uytwerf; In 's Hage, By Pieter Gosse, Jean Neaulme, Adriaan Moetjens, Antony van Dole; Te Utrecht, By Steven Neaulme, 1741–1750.

—————. *The Ambonese Curiosity Cabinet.* Translated, edited, annotated, and with an introduction by E. M. Beekman. New Haven: Yale University Press, 1999.

—————. *De Ambonese Historie. Behelsende Een kort Verhaal der Gedenkwaardigste Geschiedenissen zo in Vreede als oorlog voorgevallen sedert dat de Nederlandsche Oost Indische Comp: Het Besit in Amboina Gehadt Heeft.* In *Bijdragen tot de Taal-, Land- en Volkenkunde van Nederlandsch-Indië,* zevende volgreeks: tiende deel [vol. 64]. The Hague: Nijhoff, 1910.

—————. *Ambonsche Landbeschrijving.* Ed. Suntingan Dr. Z. J. Manusama. Jakarta: Arsip Nasional Republik Indonesia, 1983.

—————. *De Ambonse eilanden onder de VOC, zoals opgetekend in De Ambonse Landbeschrijving.* Eds. Chris van Fraassen and Hans Straver. Utrecht: Landelijk Steunpunt Educatie Molukkers, 2002.

—————. *Het Auctuarium, ofte Vermeerdering, op het Amboinsch Kruyd-boek. Dat is, Beschryving van de overige Boomen, Heesters, en Planten, die men in Amboina, en de omleggende eilanden vind, Allen zeer accuraat beschreven en afgebeeldt na der zelver gedaantes, met de verscheide Indische benamingen, aanqueking, en gebruik, door Georgius Everhardus Rumphius, Med. Doct. van Hanau, Oud Koopman en Raadspersoon in Amboina, mitsgaders onder de naam van Plinius Indicus, Lid van de Illustre Academia Naturae Curiosorum, in't Duitsche en Roomsche Ryk opgerigt. Nu voor 't eerst uitgegeven, en in het Latyn overgezet, door Joannes Burmannus, Med. Doctor, en Botanices Professor in het Illustre Athenaeum, en de Hortus Medicus te Amsteldam, Medelidt van het Keizerlyke Queekschool der onderzoekers van de Natuurkunde; Die daar verscheide Benamingen, en zyn Aanmerkingen heeft bygevoegt.* Amsterdam, By Mynard Uytwerf, en de Wed. S. Schouten en Zoon, 1755.

Schlechter, R. *The Orchidaceae of German New Guinea.* Melbourne: The Australian Orchid Foundation, 1982.

Scholes, Robert. *Semiotics and Interpretation.* New Haven: Yale University Press, 1982.

Schuiteman, A., and E. F. de Vogel. "Orchids of New Guinea, Vol. I." Amsterdam: Expert Center for Taxonomic Identification, 2001.

Sewel, William. *A New Dictionary English and Dutch, Wherein the Words are rightly interpreted, and their various significations exactly noted.* Amsterdam: By de Weduwe van Steven Swart, 1691.

Sloane, Hans. *Catalogus plantarum quae in insula Jamaica sponte proveniunt.* London: D. Brown, 1696.

————. *A voyage to the Islands Madera, Barbados, Nieves, S. Christophers and Jamaica.* 2 vols. London: printed for the author, 1707–1725.

Smith, J. J. *Die Orchideen von Ambon.* Batavia: Landsdrukkerij, 1905.

————. "The Genus Grammatophyllum." *Orchidologia Zeylanica.* Colombo, Ceylon: Orchid Circle of Ceylon. Vol. 6 (1939): 33–36.

————. "Malayan and Papuan Jewel Orchids." *The Orchid Review* 38 (January 1930): 3–9.

Sterkenburg, P. G. J. van. *Een glossarium van zeventiende-eeuws Nederlands.* 3d rev. ed. Groningen: Wolters Noordhof, 1981.

Teeuw, A. *Indonesisch-Nederlands Woordenboek.* 5th ed. Leiden: KITLV Uitgeverij, 1996.

Theophrastus. *Enguiry into Plants.* Trans. Arthur Hort. 2 vols. Loeb Classical Library. Cambridge: Harvard University Press, 1916.

Thompson, Edward Maunde. *An Introduction to Greek and Latin Palaeography* [1917]. Reprint ed., New York: Burt Franklin, 1973.

Tragi, Hieronymi. *De stirpium, maxime earum, in Germania.* Strasbourg: V. Rihelius, 1552.

Tyler, Paul. *Dutch Flower Painting 1600–1720.* New Haven: Yale University Press, 1995.

Valentijn, François. *Oud en Nieuw Oost-Indiën.* 5 books in 8 volumes. Dordrecht and Amsterdam, 1724–1726.

Valentini, M. C. *Museum Museorum.* Frankfurt am Main: Johann David Zunners, 1704.

Vermeulen, J. J. *Orchids of Borneo, Vol. 2, Bulbophyllum.* Orchids of Borneo. Sabah, Malaysia: The Sabah Society, 1997.

Vuyk Beb. *Het laatste huis van de wereld* (1939). Translated by André

Lefevere with the title *The Last House in the World* and published in *Two Tales of the East Indies.* Amherst: University of Massachusetts Press, 1983.

Wehner, U., W. Zierau, and J. Arditti. "Plinius Germanicus and Plinius Indicus: Sixteenth and seventeenth century description and illustrations of orchid 'trash baskets,' resupination, seeds, floral segments and flower senescence in European botanical literature." *Orchid Biology. Reviews and Perspectives, VIII.* Ed. T. Kull and J. Arditti. Boston: Kluwer, 2001.

Wetering, Ernst van de. *Rembrandt. The Painter at Work.* Amsterdam: Amsterdam University Press, 1997.

Wilkinson, R. J. *A Malay-English Dictionary (Romanised).* 2 vols. Reprint ed., London: Macmillan, 1959.

Wit, H. D. C. de. "Orchids in Rumphius' *Herbarium Amboinense.*" *Orchid Biology. Reviews and Perspectives, I.* Ed. Joseph Arditti. Ithaca, N.Y.: Cornell University Press, 1977.

⸻, ed. *Rumphius Memorial Volume.* Baarn: Hollandia, 1959.

Wood, J. J. *Orchids of Borneo, Vol. 3, Dendrobium, Dendrochilum and Others.* Orchids of Borneo. Sabah, Malaysia: The Sabah Society, 1997.

Wood, J. J., R. S. Beaman, and J. H Beaman. "The Plants of Mount Kinabalu, 2. Orchids." *The Plants of Mount Kinabalu.* Whitstable: Whitstable Litho, 1993, p. 411.

Wood, J. J., and P. J. Cribb. *A Checklist of the Orchids of Borneo.* Whitstable: Whitstable Litho, 1994.

Wood, Jeffrey J. "Grammatophyllum Scriptum." *The Orchid Review* (Kingsteignton, England) 8 (1977): 323–327.

Woordenboek der Nederlandsche Taal. Ed. M. de Vries and H. Heestermans, et al. 29 vols. The Hague: Martinus Nijhoff & SDU uitgeverij, 1882–1998.

Yule, Henry, and A. C. Burnell, *Hobson-Jobson: being a Glossary of Anglo-Indian colloquial words and phrases* [1886]. Reprint ed., New Delhi: Munshiram Manoharlal, 1979.

INDEX